"Ann's gentle and authentic voice welcomes readers as she points them to truth. I'm grateful for Ann's work for the kingdom through her faithful writing that points to Christ."

—Emily Jensen, co-founder of Risen Motherhood and coauthor of *Risen Motherhood: Gospel Hope for Everyday Moments*

"Ann Swindell doesn't offer empty platitudes to 'praise God anyhow'; she acknowledges the painful realities of life while displaying how the hope and truth of God's Word can grow in us the peace and strength of Christ in the least likely of places."

—Sarah Walton, coauthor of *Hope When It Hurts* and *Together Through the Storms*

"We live in a world where anxiety has become the norm and peace often feels elusive. In *The Path to Peace*, Ann Swindell offers us gospel hope through biblical teaching that redirects our hearts to Christ. This forty-day devotional will be a balm to your soul, a beacon of hope, and a declaration of God's lovingkindness that never fails for his people."

—Gretchen Saffles, bestselling author of *The Well-Watered Woman: Rooted in Truth, Growing in Grace, Flourishing in Faith*

"In a particularly confusing and loud year, the world offers us many ways to comfort ourselves and find peace, all unsatisfying. Ann shows us where to find the peace we have been promised as believers through Christ. As I read the first chapter of her honest writing, my shoulders immediately left my ears and my breathing slowed. I could not love this message more! What a hope we have in Jesus."

—Jami Nato, writer and entrepreneur

"Ann's work is tender in its vulnerability and powerful in its unwavering commitment to the gospel. Upholding the truth of God's Word while sharing from the pain in her own life, Ann's rich imagination and loving exhortations remind us that no matter our circumstances, our peace is found in God."

—Elsie Iudicello, Farmhouse Schoolhouse

"Ann Swindell's exuberant retellings of biblical narratives will capture your interest and lead you back to the Scriptures. In these God-breathed pages, we find the path to peace we desperately need."

—Megan Hill, editor of The Gospel Coalition, author of *Patience: Waiting with Hope*, pastor's wife

"When life isn't throwing us for an unexpected loop, its daily barrage of responsibilities can still threaten to steal our peace. What we need is a fresh dose of perspective gained through focused time spent with Jesus. *The Path to Peace* is a helpful resource that will calm your heart and strengthen your mind so you can meet the challenges of each day with an undisturbed heart. Highly recommended."

—Karen Ehman, author and speaker, Proverbs 31 Ministries

"I love how Ann narrows in on ordinary people of the Bible being obedient to God and doing extraordinary things, despite uncertain circumstances. We all need a good double-take at what God said when it comes to our dissatisfaction and pain."

—Alisa Keeton, founder, Revelation Wellness, author of *The Wellness Revelation*

THE
PATH
TO
PEACE

Experiencing God's Comfort
When You're Overwhelmed

ANN
SWINDELL

BETHANYHOUSE

a division of Baker Publishing Group
Minneapolis, Minnesota

Published by Bethany House Publishers
11400 Hampshire Avenue South
Bloomington, Minnesota 55438
www.bethanyhouse.com

Bethany House Publishers is a division of
Baker Publishing Group, Grand Rapids, Michigan

Printed in China

Library of Congress Cataloging-in-Publication Data
Names: Swindell, Ann, author.
Title: The path to peace : experiencing God's comfort when you're overwhelmed / Ann Swindell.
Description: Minneapolis, MN : Bethany House, a division of Baker Publishing Group, [2022]
Identifiers: LCCN 2021032915 | ISBN 9780764238895
Subjects: LCSH: Peace of mind—Religious aspects—Christianity. | Peace of mind—Biblical
    teaching. | Bible—Biography.
Classification: LCC BV4908.5 .S95 2022 | DDC 248.4—dc23
LC record available at https://lccn.loc.gov/2021032915

Cover design by Jennifer Parker

All events in this book are factual; however, some names have been changed to protect the privacy of some individuals.

Baker Publishing Group publications use paper produced from sustainable forestry practices and post-consumer waste whenever possible.

22 23 24 25 26 27 28   7 6 5 4 3 2 1

For Mom and Dad
Thank you for showing me the path to peace
that only comes through Christ. Your love for your children and
grandchildren has always mirrored the Lord's so beautifully.
I love you both.

Contents

Introduction

It was the fourth month after my husband's job loss, and I was staring at the empty fireplace of the house we thought we'd raise our kids in forever. I tried to take a deep breath, but all that came out was a shuddering wheeze.

It wasn't just the job loss or the financial stress, although that had me strung as tight as a bowstring.

It wasn't just the lack of security around our lives, our house, our future—although those had me wrung out like a wet rag.

It was the years that had piled up, full of disappointment and loss; years of failure and death and the nagging pain of foiled dreams that had crashed up against the realities of life. I was thirty minutes deep into weeping when everything in me snapped.

My tears turned to rage.

My husband, who had been rubbing my back through tears of his own, felt my spine straighten under his hands.

It came out as a whisper first. "This isn't what I signed up for."

Michael whispered back, "What did you say?"

Then it came out as a yell. The kids were in bed; the night was all around me. I yelled into the room, yelled at my husband, yelled at myself, yelled at God.

"This isn't what I signed up for! I didn't sign up for this! I didn't want this life full of transition and loss and pain! I didn't want a life with three miscarriages!" My voice escalated into the darkness. "I didn't want my son to have major medical issues! Or a life where friends turn their backs on us because we spoke the truth! I didn't want this, Michael! I hate this! This is not what I signed up for!"

An Honest Reflection

Maybe you know this feeling too? Maybe you know what it's like to look at your life and feel overwhelmed, unsure of how you got to where you are today.

None of us sign some supernatural contract for our dream life, but most of us have some vision for the kind of life we *want* to live. What I felt that night was not only sadness, but anger—and underneath that, disappointment at how my life was unfolding.

I wasn't getting what I expected from my life.

If I was honest, I wasn't getting what I expected from God.

I was shaking under the anger, my tears momentarily impeded by the force of my voice and my fists punching the couch.

Have I ever been this angry in all my life? I couldn't remember feeling this pulsing wrath before. I was erupting with years of it, here on a Tuesday night in November.

My husband moved his hand from my back and leaned toward me.

His voice was even and slow. "What do you think you signed up for?"

He does this—he leans into my hurt and my pain when I most want him to back away. I love it and hate it and need it all at the same time.

The words hung like moisture in the air, pressing down on me, suffocating my fury. My anger deflated all at once—a balloon popped by a pin.

I shook my head.

Again, he asked me, this time more gently. "Ann. What *do* you think you signed up for?"

"Not this," I whispered. I felt hot tears coming again, and I groaned; I thought I had spent them all. "I hate it. I hate this."

We were thirteen years into our marriage, and none of it looked like what I'd hoped for. Three babies lost, four moves in four and a half years, a son with a rare GI condition, abandonment from friends, a host of unusual and painful medical issues, job loss, and depression—this was not the life I had dreamed of when we promised ourselves to each other at the altar on a sunny day in May.

I had dreamed of years rooted in a house we loved, in a city we called home, with healthy children and a stable job for my husband. I had dreamed of sharing the gospel with our neighbors and hosting backyard barbeques with lifelong friends. I had dreamed of being a part of a church community that we loved and people who loved us back.

All of those dreams had been shattered. Every single one.

And I no longer wanted what I was living. I wanted someone else's life—a life that was rooted and secure, full of regular paychecks and ir-regular doctor visits and best friends who dropped by during the week just to say hi. I wanted to not think about our unclear future all the time, to not wonder what unwelcome surprise the next month might hold for our family. It felt like everyone around me had the life I wanted while we were stuck in a cycle of struggle, loss, and hurt.

How had this become our life, full of transition and trial?

"How did we get here, Michael?" I could feel that my eyes were puffy and red-rimmed, my entire face swollen with salt and tears.

He looked at me and then closed his eyes. "You know how we got here, Ann."

I did know. We'd been trying to follow God; we'd been saying yes to him. We'd been obedient. But obedience hadn't led us to a smooth life. I wasn't sure why I'd expected things to be easy just because we followed Jesus—maybe it was that I *wanted* things to be easier than they were.

We had been following the Lord, studying his Word, and obeying his call—imperfectly, of course, but earnestly. And that meant our many transitions and trials had not been due to disobedience and wandering but to saying yes to God, whose path for us had been curving and winding.

But that truth made the trials feel even harder to bear. These struggles were not due to disobedience or sin. The difficulties we were experiencing, the sorrow we had been walking through—God had allowed these hardships, and was, in fact, calling us to walk through them. This was not something we could squirm our way out of.

No. This wasn't what I thought I had signed up for.

But perhaps this was what I had agreed to after all.

The Saints Who Give Us Hope

The men and women who fill the pages of the Bible hadn't signed up for their particular stories either. Wandering through deserts, fighting giants, standing up to kings, leaving their families and homes—these are not the things most humans clamor for. These saints did not choose their own road. Instead, they chose obedience *to* and faith *in* the One who had them on it. And their yeses made all the difference.

The Bible practically trips over itself with the names and details of these kinds of women and men: Sarah and Ruth, Noah and Abraham, Mary and Paul. For many of us, these people have become more like the heroes of legend than those who could be our neighbors or friends. And indeed, these men and women accomplished great deeds and saw great miracles. But they *were* flesh and bone like us, full of their own fears and failings. Some tried to run ahead of God; some tried to go their own way. I'm sure they cried out to him in frustration and fear more times than can be counted. They longed for peace when all they felt was anxiety; they ached for rest when all they knew was toil. They faced the same emotions, dealt with the same struggles, and navigated the same responsibilities and familial tensions that we do today.

They weren't mythical legends, although we are right to consider them heroes—not solely because of their great actions, but because of their great faith.

They knew and experienced what we still do today: that holding on to faith in the Lord in the face of fear and trial is always worth it.

They knew and experienced the truth that finding peace *in* God and *with* God is worth any cost.

They knew and experienced the peace and comfort that come through faith when everything in their lives was shaken.

Peace—that seemingly elusive prize that Christ declares he has, in fact, *already* given to us in John 14:27: "Peace I leave with you; my peace I give to you. Not as the world gives do I give to you. Let not your hearts be troubled, neither let them be afraid."

When he spoke those words, Jesus knew that the lives of his disciples in every century would be full of trouble and fear, full of trials and tribulations. But he could still confidently offer us his peace. Why?

Because peace comes from our souls being at rest in God rather than in our circumstances.

Biblical Peace

While the biblical concept of peace has many connotations, a succinct and beautiful way of understanding scriptural peace is this: *Having peace means having a soul at rest in God.* Yes, peace includes emotions of tranquility and wholeness and harmony. But more than a fleeting emotion or a passing thought, peace means being at rest—being content—exactly where you are, because of who God is and because of your relationship with him through Christ.

As Christians, we can weather any storm that comes our way because we are in Christ, our refuge and peace. When the world changes and chaos threatens, Jesus Christ remains the same yesterday, today, and forever (see Hebrews 13:8). Because *he* is unchanging, we have unchanging access to peace through the shelter of his presence, no matter what we are facing. And so, peace is possible in any circumstance.

The biblical saints we will explore in the pages that follow show us, through their own circumstances and choices, that they found their truest peace in God himself. Let us allow them to point us to experiencing that same soul-at-rest peace during the seasons of life that we didn't sign up for with a God we *did* commit to—and a God who is committed and covenanted to us through the blood of his own Son.

Peace Up Ahead

What I didn't yet know on that heartbreaking night in November was that our circumstances wouldn't change for a while. And even when things did change, our life would fill with fresh trials and challenges in those new circumstances.

This is how it always is, isn't it? The lives we think we want—even think we deserve—rarely materialize the way we hope they will. We make it through one struggle only to face another. We overcome one obstacle just to hurdle another. If we are looking at our lives with the expectation of constant ease and happiness, we will constantly feel disappointed.

Years ago, I heard a pastor say that while we often expect life to be a calm sea with an occasional storm, the truth is that life is full of persistent storms—with only an occasional calm sea. Difficulties are everywhere. Trials abound. This life, as Jesus promised, has trouble. But even in what may feel like relentless trouble, Jesus also gives us this beautiful assurance: "But take heart; I have overcome the world" (John 16:33).

What a word: *overcome*. This biblical verb carries the idea of "conquering" or "carrying off the victory." Christ has conquered the world. He's carried off the victory! Alleluia! But still—what does Christ's victory mean for us, practically, in our daily lives? What does it look like for us to walk in Christ's overcoming? Because if our difficult circumstances don't always (or ever) change, how do we experience his victory in our day-to-day life?

We learn to accept his comfort in the midst of our struggles. We learn to walk in his beautiful peace.

Jesus' own words declare that this *is* possible: "Peace I leave with you; my peace I give to you. Not as the world gives do I give to you. Let not your hearts be troubled, neither let them be afraid" (John 14:27).

In the midst of trouble and fear, *this* is part of what overcoming means for us: learning to have a soul at rest even while uncontrollable realities spin like tops around us.

Trust in the Unchanging God

This is the unexpected gift that was borne out of that November season for me: *peace*. It was an unshakable peace that came from becoming rooted in Christ in a new way. For as I dove into the lives of biblical men and women in the Scriptures, I found how often God gave his people his peace. I read the Bible with a heart hungry to see God's work in and through his people and was stunned afresh by the stories of Abraham and Sarah, Noah, Hannah, Ruth, and the disciples. Every saint in the Word has their own story of unwanted trials—and also of unbounded peace in God. Time and again, I marveled at how God—whether at work in the Old Testament or in the New—offered healing and wholeness, hope, and *peace* for those who came to him. Those who looked to him for provision and grace were given just what they needed at just the right time.

My faith in the Lord began to grow, and peace settled in my soul where there had previously been only anxiety and fear. It was not because our circumstances changed; it was because the Lord was changing my heart. As I soaked in these biblical stories, I began to trust that the same God who carried Noah's family across the flood would carry us. I began to trust that the same King who provided healing for Mary Magdalene would provide healing for our hurting hearts. I couldn't see how or when these things would happen, but I *could* see that God's character was unshakable. Who he was—and is—toward his people never changes (Hebrews 13:8). Who he was for Ruth is who he is for me. Who he was for the disciples is who he is for me. It's who he is for each of his children; it's who he is for you.

Once I started to grasp this amazing reality that the Scriptures proclaim at every turn, my soul was able to begin to truly rest. I was comforted because I knew God was in control; I knew the same God who delivered countless saints of old would surely deliver me.

As you read the passages of Scripture that the stories in these chapters reference, and as you see how God's people responded to his work in their lives and in the world, my hope is that your own faith will be stirred. My prayer is that your soul will start to experience the peace of knowing that the same God who sustained our brothers and sisters in the Bible is doing the same for you—even right now, even today.

How to Read this Book

This devotional is made up of eight sections, and each section has five daily readings in the form of chapters. A great way to read this book is to start with section 1 and read a devotion on the days you desire, moving through the chapters in order. Alternatively, you can pick a section that resonates with your current life situation and start there! I would recommend reading the chapters of each section in order, but the sections themselves can be read in any order you want.

You will get the most benefit from this book if you take the time to read the Scripture passages that are noted at the start of each chapter. While the words I offer in these devotions have been thoughtfully and prayerfully written, the truth is that *nothing* transforms us as much as the Word of God. Reading the Bible is what our hearts need most.

More than anything else, I pray that the stories and reflections in these pages will awaken your love for Christ and his Word!

SECTION 1

· ·

SARAH

Peace in a New Calling

DAYS 1–5

DAY 1

Peace through Trusting God's Path

*The LORD had said to Abram, "Go from your country, your
people and your father's household to the land I will show you."*

Genesis 12:1 NIV

• **Read Genesis 12:1-5** •

Sarai kept her eyes closed. If she opened them, she was afraid that this might not be a dream from which she could awaken and escape.

"Sarai? Did you not hear me?" Abram's voice was filled with confusion.

Sarai allowed herself one more moment before opening her eyes. Abram had moved closer—too close—and his beard was nearly scratching her chin.

"Ah! Abram!" She swatted him.

His eyes crinkled at the corners and he softened. "I was worried you had fallen asleep."

"Sleep? After what you just told me? I may never be able to sleep again!" Abram stepped back and Sarai rose from the pallet on the floor, her body protesting the quick movement. She stood as tall as she could and balled her fists on her hips, narrowing her gaze. "Tell me, Abram. Who is 'the Lord'? Who is this voice you have heard, calling us to leave all we have here in Harran? And where will we go?" She raised her eyebrows. "Did he tell you a *place* to go? Or even an arrow to point the way?"

Abram's chest rose and fell. He said nothing.

Sarai answered his silence with her own.

After several beats, Abram spoke. "I will tell you what I have already said—all that I heard from Yahweh. We are to leave our land, our people, and this house of my father's. We are to go where he sends us, and he will bless me and make of me a great nation." He hesitated, then coughed. "And the Lord said that all people on earth will be blessed . . . through me."

Now it was Sarai's turn to take a deep breath. Abram had never been a prideful man, but neither was he particularly humble. He loved his flocks and his herds, his home and his household. But to think that the entire world would be blessed because of him? She huffed. He had to be making at least some of this up . . . didn't he?

She opened her mouth to speak, but Abram stopped her with a hand on her shoulder. "Sarai. My love." His eyes were pleading. "I know how this must sound to you. I know you must think me crazy. I know that this is not anything that we had planned. But I can tell you this: I have heard from God." There was steadfastness in his eyes, and a determination she had not seen before. "I will not—I dare not—disobey." He raised his chin. "I trust him."

Sarai matched his gaze and knew, then, that her husband had made his decision. She also knew, somehow, that he was telling the truth. The Lord, whoever he was, was God. Abram was going. She could now agree and help him, or fight him all the way. But how she responded would not change his actions. She could see that.

She blinked back her tears. "All right, my husband." She turned to fold the linens. "When do we leave?"

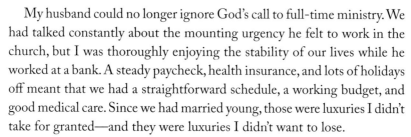

My husband could no longer ignore God's call to full-time ministry. We had talked constantly about the mounting urgency he felt to work in the church, but I was thoroughly enjoying the stability of our lives while he worked at a bank. A steady paycheck, health insurance, and lots of holidays off meant that we had a straightforward schedule, a working budget, and good medical care. Since we had married young, those were luxuries I didn't take for granted—and they were luxuries I didn't want to lose.

But when our church came to Michael and offered him a position on staff, he felt that this was what God had been calling him to. The catch? No income for the first three to six months, no health insurance, and a ministry schedule of nights and weekends. The position would require us to raise support until the church grew enough to pay us—and even then, nothing was guaranteed.

This was everything I *didn't* want.

I loved our tidy life. I loved the clarity of knowing what our weeks and bank account looked like. I loved the ability to travel on the weekends, even if that meant missing church once in a while. And I knew that taking this ministry position would change all of that.

But Michael believed this opportunity was God's path for us, and I could see that his heart was already set on moving into the pastoral role. The timing, the overwhelming support from our family and friends and church leadership—all of it pointed to this being God's plan for us.

It just wasn't what *I* had planned.

Even if Sarai believed that Abram was telling the truth, I imagine that she still struggled with what that calling required of her. It wasn't what she had planned for her life. She probably still had dreams of having children, of raising a family, and of seeing her own grandchildren settled in the family home—not of traipsing across the desert to an unknown destination.

Often, other people make decisions that radically impact our lives. For example, while none of us chose the way we were parented, the effects of that parenting—for good or ill—stay with us even as adults. A boss that hires us (or fires us) can impact our financial stability overnight. A spouse who remains faithful—or doesn't—holds great power over the dynamics of trust in our marriage. And a child who stays the course or strays from it can alter family relationships forever.

While most of us want to maintain control over our own lives, we have all deeply felt the reality that we cannot control everything—or even most things—in our world. We often feel overwhelmed by the sheer number of details we cannot alter.

Sarai lived this reality as well. After one encounter with God, her husband turned their entire lives around. Everything she had known, every way that she had built her life—all of it was gone in an instant because of what Abram heard from God. As a wife in the ancient world, that meant that the decision had been made for her: Abram's calling became her own. So Sarai also had a choice to make: Would she follow the Lord willingly into a calling that she hadn't chosen, or would she fight it all the way?

A choice had been made. Now it was up to her to decide how to respond.

My husband's call to full-time ministry meant a different life for me too. It meant learning to be a pastor's wife, living on a much smaller income, and having less flexibility with our schedule, among countless other things. They felt like huge changes at the time, and I wrestled with them.

But as we continued to pray and talk with others, it became obvious that full-time ministry *was* God's path for us. And when we accepted the job and joined the church staff, what I experienced was great peace. My soul was content, knowing that we were obeying God's will.

This is what we see in Scripture: Obedience to God leads to peace with God.

Psalm 119 points out this intermingling of obedience to God and the experience of his peace:

> Great peace have those who love your law,
> and nothing can make them stumble.
> I wait for your salvation, LORD,
> and I follow your commands.
> I obey your statutes,
> for I love them greatly.
> I obey your precepts and your statutes,
> for all my ways are known to you.
>
> vv. 165–168 NIV

The psalmist here is highlighting that loving God's law and obeying it brings great peace. For us, while there was no verse in the Bible that told us we should go into full-time ministry, the church job aligned with prayer, circumstances, and the collective voice of God's people around us. This was our path.

And so I made the choice to agree with God's calling rather than fight against it. I chose to trust that as I obeyed him, I would experience the blessing of his peace—of having a soul at rest in God.

Obedience to God leads to peace with God.

That has proven true a thousand times over. There would be years when I could not yet see where life in ministry would cause immense joy and also unfathomable pain. But through it all, I have known the peace of God—that this is where we are supposed to be, even in the hard times.

Many of us will find ourselves in circumstances that we cannot change, and in new callings we didn't choose. Sarai certainly did. She didn't have any power to force Abram to ignore God. She couldn't stay put while her husband packed up the house and followed God into the desert.

But each of us can choose our response to the life that we have been given, right now. By loving God's Word and obeying him, we can experience his peace, regardless of the circumstance in front of us. Will it always be easy? Hardly. But following God leads to experiencing the peace of God that gives our souls rest, no matter what we face.

● **REFLECT:** How can you choose to obey God in the midst of the circumstances you find yourself in today? Ask God to help you obey his Word and experience his peace as you do so.

DAY 2

Peace as We Trust God's Protection

"Now then, here is your wife; take her, and go."
Genesis 12:19

● Read Genesis 12:10–20 ●

They had been traveling more days than Sarai could count. Sand nestled in every crevice of clothing she had with her, no matter how many times she shook them out.

But Yahweh had met with Abram again and had promised the land of Canaan to him and to his children. *Children!* Sarai had thrilled at the words as Abram relayed them to her. How desperately she had hoped for children in her younger years. But still, her womb remained empty.

And now her stomach was empty too. There was a famine, and both the herds and the people in their caravan were getting perilously low on food stores. She reached into the bag of grain and did the mental calculations: They could make it another two weeks if they stretched every resource they had. The herds were growing lean—as was her husband.

As if on cue, Abram threw back the tent flap and ran a hand through his beard. "We must go to Egypt, my love. Today. They have grain."

—※—

Days later, with the land of Egypt sprawling before them, Abram came up on his camel and found her.

He caressed her cheek. "You are a beautiful woman, Sarai. When the Egyptians see you, they will assume you are my wife, and they will want you for their own. They will take you and kill me."

"Abram! No such thing will happen!" But there was ice down her spine.

His voice was full of sadness. "We must tell them you are my sister; then my life will be spared."

"But if they think I am your sister—" Sarai's mind spiraled down. Her hands began to shake uncontrollably. "Abram. They—they will take me for their own!"

He could not look her in the face. "I am sorry." There were tears streaming into his beard.

It was as her husband said. Before she knew it, Abram had told the Egyptians his lie, and they had whisked Sarai away to become part of Pharaoh's harem.

—※—

Several years ago, my husband was fired from a pastoral position for speaking the truth.

My anger flamed at the injustice of it all. Church was supposed to be where truth was upheld! Instead, my husband had been punished. But my anger was tempered by fear, because we had lost not only our family's main income, but also our entire church community. And as the pain of what had happened impacted every area of our lives, my strong, confident husband spiraled into depression.

I took on the burden of feeling like I had to hold the family together. I still had a my job, but I needed to work more to keep our family afloat. Michael was so depressed that he was nearly nonfunctional some days, and I had to try and meet our family's practical needs in the midst of my own emotional turmoil. Meals, laundry, consistent bedtimes for the kids, switching health insurance plans—all of it fell to me.

On my better days, I was peaceful and hope-filled. But most days, I was exhausted, overwhelmed, and afraid.

⸺⸻

When Abram lied to protect himself in Egypt, Sarai bore the brunt of his lie. He knew that she might be sent to Pharaoh's harem to be one of his concubines, but he probably also felt that he had no choice—they were starving to death in the desert, and Egypt was the only place with food. So Abram chose to ultimately protect himself rather than his wife (see verse 13). Sarai must have felt both terrified and furious; she was in a strange land with no resources at her disposal.

There was only one person now who could help her—Yahweh, whom her husband had been telling her about. Had Sarai ever heard the Lord or seen him for herself? Abram was the one who received the visions and desert moments with God; the Scriptures don't tell us if she was a part of those experiences. But still, I wonder if Sarai started praying while she was in Egypt, asking this God she did not yet know to help her.

She had nowhere else to turn.

⸺⸻

In those bleak months after Michael lost his job, I spent a great deal of time praying, and it was because I had nowhere else to go. My husband was deep in darkness. Most of our church friends had abandoned us. I bucketed out my heart to the Lord, pouring out tears and prayers at his feet. I told him how worried I was about Michael's mental health, how scared I was about our financial situation, how lonely I felt, how I couldn't see any clarity for what was ahead.

God was the only one I could fully turn to—and he met me.

Over and over, I experienced the Lord protecting us in unexpected ways—and giving me his comfort and peace in the process. A college friend offered us free legal services. A family member sent us a check in the mail. Our kids made new friends. Our counselors helped us work through deep hurts. We had a small handful of friends that stuck closer than brothers. And God upheld Michael's reputation even as others spoke untrue stories about him. These were things only the Lord could do for us—and he did. He shielded and protected us in our weakness and need and emotional pain.

As he did so, we knew his peace.

The Lord protected Sarai too. He shielded and protected her from having to become Pharaoh's concubine in a way she could not have expected: "The Lord afflicted Pharaoh and his house with great plagues because of Sarai, Abram's wife" (Genesis 12:17). God saw what was happening, and when Sarai could not defend herself, he did it for her—not just barely, but with "great plagues" on her behalf.

> Whatever you face today, the Lord sees you and is protecting you.

God became her protector. He showed himself mighty *for her.*

Sarai, who had not yet had her own encounter with Yahweh, now knew that God saw her and was protecting her as well. What a balm this must have been to her heart! What peace she must have felt, knowing that God was not just looking out for Abram, but that *she* was also known and chosen by him!

In Sarai's calling as the wife of Abram, she faced multiple trials and troubles. Her time in Egypt was one of those trials. Still, the Lord saw what she faced, and he protected her. In fact, when Sarai was freed from Pharaoh's house, she left not only with her husband and their flocks and herds, but with the food they needed too.

Know that whatever you face today, the Lord sees you and is protecting you. It may not feel like protection right now—you may be walking into Pharaoh's palace, feeling alone and scared—but God is never late with his protection and provision. Call on him today and pray that he will protect, shield, and carry you—and go forward in peace, knowing that he will.

- **REFLECT:** Where do you need God's protection right now? Ask him to show himself mighty on your behalf and give you his peace, knowing that he sees you and will shield you.

DAY 3

No Peace When We Try to Force Our Calling

And he brought him outside and said, "Look toward heaven,
and number the stars, if you are able to number them."
Then he said to him, "So shall your offspring be."

Genesis 15:5

• Read Genesis 15:1–6; 16:1–6 •

The words came out like dust in Sarai's mouth. "The Lord has prevented me from bearing children."

Abram's voice resonated with confidence. "The Lord spoke to me, saying, 'Your very own son shall be your heir.' He called me to look at the heavens and told me our offspring shall be as numerous as the stars, Sarai. He will fulfill his word."

Sarai's legs suddenly felt weak. "I do not doubt what he told you, husband." And she didn't. She was learning to believe what the Lord said. "But he did not say that the child would be *my* son—just that he would be *yours*."

She let the silence hang for a moment. No matter the promises Abram heard from the Lord, the truth was that she was still barren.

Her heart begged her not to do it, but Sarai forced herself to spit out the next words. "Take Hagar as your wife; maybe I will get children through her."

Abram looked down, and her fears pooled in her chest as a wave ready to overtake her. While she knew this was the most logical way—women did this all the time with their handmaids, claiming the babe as their own—she still wanted Abram to fight her. He had only ever been faithful.

But he did not protest. Perhaps he saw, like she did, that this was what they should do.

Even if she hated it.

<hr>

At some point or another, most of us will feel the desire to try and force our own plans rather than trusting in what God has planned for us. For me, one of those times came through a new writing opportunity with an organization I loved. I was *convinced* that I could handle this; it would be such an incredible chance for my career!

Never mind that I had a full work schedule already. Never mind that it was unpaid. Never mind that my husband had just started a new pastoral position and I had responsibilities as a pastor's wife. Never mind that our son was wrestling with a challenging medical condition and every day felt like a minor emergency with him. I *wanted* to take this writing opportunity, and I felt that, for my career, I *needed* to take it.

Michael didn't agree. In most things in my life and work, Michael is my biggest cheerleader: he encourages me, helps me brainstorm, and takes the kids on adventures on his days off so that I can write. But he could see burnout coming at me like a freight train and told me so.

Still, I argued. I protested. I got desperate to take this chance—and I took it anyway.

It didn't go well.

The work was more intensive than I expected it to be, and soon I was stressed out and anxious because of it. Peace evaporated from our home. I snapped at my kids, complained to Michael about how overwhelmed I was, and struggled to take a Sabbath. The months wore on, and the extra work wore me out.

I had been trying to force my way into professional success, and it was hurting our family. After a particularly stressful month full of work and deadlines that I could hardly meet, I owned up to the fact that taking this opportunity was *not* God's best for me. In fact, it had never been his best for me—I just hadn't been willing to listen and trust him when it *seemed* so perfect. I tried to force my calling into existence because I couldn't see any other way of getting what I wanted.

When Sarai offered her handmaid, Hagar, to Abram as a way of getting a son through her, Sarai was trying to force her calling into existence. She gave up waiting on God by doing what culture told her was normal because she couldn't see any other way of getting what she wanted. Knowing her age and her barrenness, Sarai could not fathom how else to get a child, and so she tried to force the calling on her life—and Abram's—by making her own plans.

But trying to force her calling did not bring the peace she craved. Instead, when Hagar became pregnant with Abram's son, Hagar came to hate her mistress, and her attitude enraged Sarai. Tension erupted in Sarai and Abram's marriage (see Genesis 16:5–6), and Sarai was so harsh with her maidservant that Hagar ran away. Anger, frustration, pain, violence—this was the outcome of Sarai trying to fulfill her own calling rather than trusting God to do that for her.

She couldn't see what the Lord had ahead for her, so she tried to force his will in her own way.

When I have tried to force my own calling rather than trusting God to do his work, the result has been similar: frustration, pain, and anger.

God works in his way and in his timing in our lives—and his purpose and calling for us will come to fruition when we walk in step with him. But when we act on what we think is best and try to force our vision for our lives into reality, the outcome will be the same: frustration, pain, and relational tension.

The opposite of peace.

If there is any place in your life today where you feel overwhelmed or desperate to make things happen through your own volition or strength, step back and ask God to help you see things as he does. If he is asking you to wait and trust in him, ask

> God works in his way and in his timing—and his purpose for us will come to fruition when we walk in step with him.

him for the peace and faith to do that. It is hard to wait on God's timing: like Sarai, we want to see him work *now*. But God's will shall be accomplished in and through us as we trust him rather than forcing our own plan.

And take heart: If you have already rushed ahead of God, there is grace to repent and turn to the Lord. As the apostle Paul reminds us, although Sarai lacked faith in this choice with Hagar, she did not stay in a place of unbelief. In fact, she is hailed as one of the saints whose faith was deep and true: "By faith Sarah herself received power to conceive, even when she was past the age, since she considered him faithful who had promised" (Hebrews 11:11).

Although Sarai at one time tried to push ahead of God and force her calling, she grew in her faith and came to trust that God was faithful, and that his calling in her life would come to pass. The same can be true of us: we can grow in our faith as we ask God to help us walk in peace while we trust in him!

- **REFLECT:** Where do you need to trust God with your calling? What promises are you waiting for him to fulfill? Pray that he will give you the strength to trust his timing and purpose for your life—and that you will have his peace as you wait on him.

DAY 4

Peace When Our Calling
Seems Impossible

Is anything too hard for the LORD?
Genesis 18:14

• Read Genesis 18:9–15 •

The tent flap blew open and Abraham stormed in. "Quick!" His voice was a low whisper. "Three seahs of fine flour! Knead it and make cakes!" Without another word, he flew back out.

Sarah followed his path to the flap and peeked out. Her husband had left just moments ago to talk with the three men under the oak trees, not far from their door. *Who are they?*

She rolled the image of them through her mind as she worked the flour beneath her hands. She had never seen them before, but they intrigued her. They did not look like most men. They were extraordinary men. Unusual.

The other thing that was unusual was trying to get used to her new name—and Abraham's. The Lord had changed her husband's name from "exalted father" to "father of multitudes"—still that same promise they had been clinging to for over twenty years. Apparently, God hadn't forgotten the promise that they would have many descendants. Sarah shook her head. Even the possibility of children was gone now—her cycles had ended years ago.

She kneaded the flour into small balls, adding oil until she could flatten them under her palm. Soon the cakes emerged from the fire, browned and warm. Abraham came back in and, without a word, scooped them into a bowl and hurried out again. His eyes were huge.

Sarah stood at the tent entrance, listening.

"Where is Sarah, your wife?" The voice felt as close as her own breath. Her heart kicked in her chest.

"She is in the tent." That was Abraham.

And then that resonant voice again: "I will surely return to you about this time next year, and Sarah, your wife, shall have a son."

Sarah laughed out loud. Who was this man, thinking she could be pregnant? *He does not know me!* She spoke under her breath in a whisper: "After I am worn out, and my lord is old, shall I have pleasure?"

And then she froze.

"Why did Sarah laugh and say, 'Shall I indeed bear a child, now that I am old?' Is anything too hard for the Lord? At the appointed time, I will return to you, about this time next year, and Sarah shall have a son."

That voice. It felt like it was with her in this very room!

She stepped into the light of the doorway, desperate to defend herself, blurting the first thing that came to mind. "I-I did not laugh!"

One of the men looked at her with a twinkle in his eye. "No, but you *did* laugh."

There was not anger there, as she expected, but . . . amusement? Joy, even?

Sarah nearly fell backward into the tent, catching herself before collapsing on the floor. *Who are these men?*

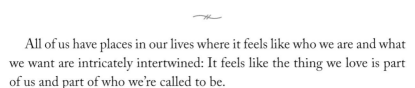

All of us have places in our lives where it feels like who we are and what we want are intricately intertwined: It feels like the thing we love is part of us and part of who we're called to be.

Maybe for you it's painting or gardening. Maybe it's running your own business, singing, or running 5k's. Maybe it's getting married or becoming a mom.

For as long as I can remember, I have wanted to be a writer. I was writing stories in blank books in elementary school, submitting poetry for the literary journal in high school, and piling up writing degrees in college and grad school well into my twenties. And while I had some success writing articles, stories, and essays, what I really wanted to do was author a book.

The problem was that I kept getting rejected in the one area I really longed for success. I sent out book proposal after book proposal, and every time I heard the same response: no.

I had been working on and sending out book proposals for over eight years. And over and over and over again: no, no, no.

Spiritually and emotionally, it was exhausting—and my soul was restless. I lost my peace in my work as a writer, and I got to the place where I was afraid to try again.

I think this is a feeling many of us experience: We have tried and failed so many times that trying again feels too tender. Another failure might break our hearts—or steal any shred of peace we have left.

So we just stop trying.

Sarah knew what rejection and fear felt like. For decades—the whole of her marriage—she had been longing for a child. And when Hagar got pregnant easily and quickly by her husband, Sarah learned that she *was* the problem, not Abraham. To add insult to injury, her cycle had stopped. There was no physical way she could actually conceive a child anymore.

So when the Lord appeared to Abraham under the oak trees, Sarah was not in a place, emotionally or spiritually, to hear anything new about being a mother. In her mind, her time had passed.

But the Lord is not bound by our time or our ways—or by our physical limitations.

His declaration that Sarah would be holding a child in her arms within the year was absolutely true, even though Sarah could not comprehend it. Is it any surprise that she laughed at such a declaration? With her history, it would have sounded absurd!

What God pronounces will happen— no matter how impossible it seems.

But *nothing* is too hard for the Lord. Barren wombs, worn-out bodies, broken dreams, unfulfilled longings—these are not roadblocks for him.

What God pronounced would happen—no matter how impossible it seemed.

―※―

Unlike Sarah, most of us will have no specific biblical promise from the Lord that what we long for will come to pass. Whether it's to see our talent recognized in the eyes of the world, to have our familial dreams come true, or for something else entirely, we have no Word-from-God guarantee of these things here on earth.

But what *is* guaranteed is something far better: peace on the journey with Christ. As we stay faithful to what God has called us to do, right now, in this moment, we can have a soul that is at rest in God, knowing that whatever we are praying for, nothing is too hard for the Lord. He will do what is best, in his way and his timing.

Yes, if he can cause a ninety-year-old barren woman to give birth to a son, he can do anything! Still, our responsibility is not to figure out *how* he will accomplish good works in our lives; it is to stay faithful and obedient to him in the journey. Don't give up on following Jesus. Don't give in to despair or anger.

With God, all things are possible. Today, we can walk in peace as we cling to his ability to accomplish his will in and through us.

• **REFLECT:** What aspect of your life feels impossible right now? Where do you lack the peace of knowing that God is in control? Ask him to remind your heart of his ability—and that nothing is too hard for him.

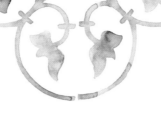

DAY 5

Peace When God Fulfills His Promise

And Sarah conceived and bore Abraham a son in his old age
at the time of which God had spoken to him.

Genesis 21:2

• **Read Genesis 21:1–7** •

Sarah was laughing so hard that she had to wipe the tears from her chin. "Who could have imagined such a thing?" The child was a boy, strong and screaming. She held him close and let the laughter overtake her, mingling now with tears of gratitude. "My bones are as old as the dirt, and yet this dead womb has brought forth new life!"

The midwives, half a life younger than Sarah, were just as astonished. They giggled with her even as they ministered to her, cleaning her and the floor where she had just brought forth her son.

Abraham came in as soon as the midwives told him he could.

"My son! My wife! Oh, Sarah!" He raised the boy into the air so quickly that his swaddle fell off, and their boy screamed in his father's arms, naked and startled.

Abraham started laughing, first with a chuckle, and then with huge belly laughs that finally stunned the child into silence. "Isaac! You came into this world with laughter—for you have brought joy to your mother and to me. And to the Lord, I imagine! Oh, God, how we thank you for this child!"

He turned his gaze to Sarah and his glistening eyes softened. "And how I thank you for my wife, who has borne me a son at the age of one hundred!" He laughed again, and Isaac began to cry.

Sarah reached out her arms, aching for the child she hardly believed was real. He suckled as soon as he was on her chest.

"God has made laughter for me." Sarah shook her head in amazement. "Everyone who hears will laugh over me!" She leaned back, more content and happy than she could ever remember. "And why should they not? It is too wonderful to be true."

—✳—

We were at the Saint Louis Zoo, waiting for the phone call that was going to determine our future. After walking through unemployment, depression, and relational pain, we were at the tail end of a twelve-week-long interview process with a church halfway across the country. We were hoping—and had been dearly praying—that this was God's plan for us, as every other door had closed. Michael had already gone through multiple rounds of interviews with the staff and elders. They had flown both of us to the church, and he had preached to the entire congregation two weeks beforehand. The last step was for the congregation to vote on whether or not to offer him the job.

The vote took place on the Sunday between Christmas and New Year's Day, when we were traveling to see family over the holiday break. Neither of us was up to driving through the night, so we stayed in a hotel in St. Louis and woke up in the city on Sunday, looking for anything to keep our minds off of what we couldn't control—the congregational vote. We decided to take the kids to the zoo.

After meandering through the penguin exhibit and gawking at the majestic polar bear through a wall of glass, we strolled through the safari section. The gorillas sat and ate, and the rhinos stared us down across the yards. I suggested that we keep walking, trying to ignore the time. The vote should have finished by now.

Michael's phone buzzed as we stood in front of the elephants. I held my breath and watched his face as he took the call.

"Hello?"

Pause.

"Hi! Yes."

Another pause.

"That's fantastic!" He gave me a huge thumbs-up. "We're thrilled!"

Tears came to my eyes as my husband's face broke into a smile. I don't remember what else he said, just that as soon as he ended the call, both of us began laughing—and laughing and laughing.

There in front of the elephants, the stress and pressure we had carried for most of the year melted into joyful laughter. Our kids joined in the laughing as we all hugged and jumped up and down. The Lord had provided for us! We couldn't stop laughing and yelling and praising him, even as others gave us sideways glances.

I realized, there at the zoo, that peace sounded a lot like laughter that day.

We purchased a stuffed elephant before leaving, which Michael keeps propped up in his office. It reminds us of God's faithfulness and the way that he met us there—with his peace and his laughter—at the Saint Louis Zoo.

If you've ever felt anything like what Sarah did when Isaac was born—or what our family felt when my husband got a new job after a season of unemployment and loss—you know that joy and laughter are the natural response of a heart set free.

"A joyful heart is good medicine," the Bible reminds us (Proverbs 17:22). Joy, laughter, praise—these things heal our hearts more than any physical medicine can. In seasons of pain and loss, joy and laughter may be hard to come by. But for all of us, there *is* an ultimate season of joy up ahead.

Because no matter what you face today, there is a final day coming when Christ will return and there will be no more tears—only joy: "He will wipe every tear from their eyes. There will be no more death or mourning or crying or pain, for the old order of things has passed away" (Revelation 21:4 NIV).

Yes, when God fulfills a promise in our lives, the right response is praise and joy and laughter! But even if we live in a long season without seeing God bring about change—even if, like Sarah, we wait until we are ninety for the fulfillment of his promise in our lives—even now, we can walk in peace.

Why? Because God is making all things new (Revelation 21:5). He is in the process of redeeming and restoring our stories. He is at work in our lives, in ways seen and unseen. And that is why—even today—we can have souls that are at rest in him.

> Joy and laughter are the natural response of a heart set free.

- **REFLECT:** Can you praise God for how he has brought laughter and fulfilled promises into your life? In what area of your life are you still waiting on him? No matter where you find yourself, there is peace in knowing that there is a season of pure joy ahead—one with Christ that will never end.

MOSES

Peace in an Unwanted Role

DAYS 6–10

DAY 6

Coming with Fear and Finding Peace in His Presence

And God said, "I will be with you."
Exodus 3:12

● **Read Exodus 3:1–12** ●

The sand was warm under his feet, but his entire body went cold with the shock of fear.

Before him, a bush was overcome with licks of flame. And the closer Moses looked, the more he was astonished: The bush was burning but unharmed.

Where am I?

Then a voice—one booming like a waterfall but tender as love—filled the air with a weightiness that drove Moses to his knees.

"Moses! Moses!"

His own voice came out as a whisper. "Here I am." He felt his hands shake as they spread before him in the sand.

"Do not come any closer." The magnificent voice pulsed through his body and his heart like a drum. "Take off your sandals, for the place where you are standing is holy ground."

Moses shifted his weight to reach behind him and tore off the leather straps. He waited, afraid to move.

The voice vibrated through and around him again. "I am the God of your father, the God of Abraham, the God of Isaac, and the God of Jacob."

Moses gasped, covering his face with his hands as his forehead dropped to the desert floor. He could feel the granules of sand in his hair and wondered if this would be his last moment on earth.

He was terrified.

———

Have you ever felt terrified? Not just afraid, but really, truly terrified? Perhaps you thought you were going to die, or perhaps you came face-to-face with your greatest fear?

For me, one of these moments happened when I experienced my first anaphylactic reaction. I was in my early thirties when my palms and the bottoms of my feet suddenly turned red and alive with inflammation and itchiness. I needed to fall down or throw up—I couldn't tell which. The walls around me whirled and surged as I began to black out. My body was completely out of my control.

After an ambulance ride and several hours at the ER, I quickly found an allergist. I now carry an EpiPen with me wherever I go. Fear motivated me to get the help I needed.

———

Moses: the baby in the basket. Moses: the prince of Egypt. Moses: the man with arms aloft while a wall of sea flanks in front of him. Moses: a lone figure carrying two tablets etched by the very finger of God.

However we might think of Moses when his name comes up, it is easy to remember him in the middle of miraculous stories. He's the beautiful child, the chosen one, the mighty leader. In children's Bibles and devotionals, in movies and soundtracks, Moses' story is full of the flashy moments: the plagues in Egypt, the exodus of God's people, the parting of the Red Sea, the provision of manna in the desert. We recall on his start as a babe in a basket and his adoptive royal mother; at every turn, his life seems incredible.

But his was also a life marked by fear.

Moses felt immense fear when he came upon the presence of God in the desert—and with good reason. In the Old Testament, we learn that no one could see the face of God and live (Exodus 33:20). Moses was afraid for his life.

But fear is actually a gift to us, for it can help us when we respond to it rightly. For Moses, that meant stripping off his sandals, falling to his knees, and listening. For me, that meant finding a doctor and getting emergency medicine.

In whatever circumstance you find yourself today, know that any fear you experience is meant to strengthen you to get the help you need. And while that help may come in the form of a doctor or medicine or a counselor or a friend, what the human heart *ultimately* needs is the peace that comes from the presence of God. Why? Because God is our greatest Helper (Psalm 118:7; John 14:26). When it comes to getting help, our supreme help always comes from him.

Yes—that same Presence that scared Moses is actually the antidote to his fear as well. The presence of God becomes his help.

For while God is mighty and awesome (and we should rightly fear his holiness!), he is also humble and lowly. The God whose presence alarmed Moses in the desert is the same one who came as the baby born in a manger. The same God whose existence emblazoned the bush also hugged children and touched lepers and ate with sinners. He knew Moses and called him by name; he knows you and calls you by name too.

And although it is God's very presence that frightens Moses, it is also actually what saves him: God *overcomes* Moses' fear with his presence. For as he calls Moses into a new role—as the leader of the Israelites—Moses is deeply afraid. God's answer to him? "I will be with you" (Exodus 3:12). God would be with Moses, and that truth offered him peace.

God's presence is what gives us peace when we come face-to-face with our fears.

God's presence is what gives us peace when we come face-to-face with our fears. He is the antidote to our fear, not because our fears disappear (Moses still had to lead his people), but because we don't face them alone. His *presence* is our help in times of trouble (Psalm 46:1).

If you are a believer in Christ, whatever fear you are facing today—and no matter what role you must carry out in your life—you are not alone. *Immanuel is with you.* Christ has promised to "be with you forever" (see John 14:16–17).

His presence with you, through the great gift of the Holy Spirit, is the help that you need to overcome fear and experience peace—the peace of a soul that is at rest in God and with God, knowing that you are never alone.

- **REFLECT:** Ask God to help you better understand his presence with you today. How is he with you in the midst of your circumstances? How is he helping you? Write down what comes to mind, and ask him for the peace that comes from knowing you are never alone. And if you don't feel him right now? You can rely on Scripture—read John 14:6-7.

DAY 7

Peace in Accepting God's Plan

But Moses said, "Pardon your servant, Lord.
Please send someone else."

Exodus 4:13 NIV

• **Read Exodus 4:10–17** •

As Moses kept his face in the sand, he heard that beautiful and awesome voice—the voice of God—telling him that he was going to free the Israelites from Egypt. What should have been thrilling news weighed Moses down like lead, for it meant that he was going to have to be the one to tell Pharaoh to let God's people go.

Moses trembled. *I can't go back.* Even as the words of God thundered in his mind and body, competing thoughts of his own rumbled just as loudly. *I cannot go back to Egypt. If they don't kill me first, Pharaoh certainly won't listen to me. I can hardly string five words together without stumbling over my speech! I can't do this! I don't want this!*

The voice of God was quiet. And into the silence, Moses' own words came stuttering out, his hands still covering his eyes.

"P-p-pardon your servant, Lord. I have n-n-never been eloquent, n-n-neither in the p-past nor since you have spoken to your s-s-servant. I am slow of speech and—and tongue."

The voice of God was immovable. "Who gave human beings their mouths? Who makes them deaf or mute? Who gives them sight or makes them blind? Is it not I, the Lord? Now go; I will help you speak and will teach you what to say."

But Moses was desperate for a way out. "P-p-pardon your servant, Lord. *Please* send s-s-someone else!"

Now the Lord's voice turned fiery, and Moses curled his body up as tightly as he could against what he was sure would be sudden death.

"What about your brother, Aaron the Levite? I know he can speak well. You shall speak to him and put words in his mouth; I will help both of you speak and will teach you what to do. He will speak to the people for you, and it will be as if he were your mouth and as if you were God to him. But take this staff in your hand so you can perform the signs with it."

Moses exhaled slowly and knew that he must relent. There would be no getting out of this.

⁕

A couple years ago, in the middle of trying to figure out our son's rare gastrointestinal condition, I woke up most days with heart palpitations and tears already pooling in my eyes. I was afraid for Judah's life; at four months old, every food that entered his body through my milk made him sicker and sicker.

I was also worried about what his illness meant for our family as a whole: How would our marriage hold up with a child who could be ill long-term? How would our daughter fare when her brother was getting so much of the attention? And how long would my own body be able to sustain this? As Judah's sole source of nutrition, I was on a deeply restricted diet. At one point, under the care of a doctor, I was down to eating only four foods to help my son survive. Yes—only four. It was extreme.

Every day felt heavy and impossible to slog through. Judah was up crying and grunting and screaming for hours every night, constantly in pain. I woke up each morning deeply anxious, unsure if I could emotionally make it through another day. I didn't want to do it.

When it came down to it, I didn't want the life I had; I didn't want the role I had been given.

But I had to relent to the life in front of me. I had no other choice! No one else could be Judah's mom; very basically, no one else could nurse him. If anyone was going to do a total elimination diet for Judah, it was going to be me. If anyone was going to hold him in his pain during the middle of the night or navigate his medical care, it was going to be one of two people—me or my husband. There was no way out. I felt trapped by my own life, and I prayed and prayed that God would heal our son and change our reality.

I imagine that Moses felt trapped too—trapped in a life story he didn't want or ask for. Scripture shows us that he pleaded with God to let him off the hook. But rather than yielding, God reminds Moses that he is in charge of everything—even Moses' very body—and that he will help him do what he is called to do.

Moses begs *one more time* to get out of the assignment. In response, God gives him a human helper in Aaron.

But still, the Lord offers him no way out.

This was the plan God had for him. There was no other option.

At three and a half years old, Judah is now doing incredibly well, and I am deeply thankful. But do I understand why my son's health has been so difficult? No. Do I still pray every day that God will fully heal him? Absolutely. Still, in the midst of this journey with our son, I have been able to experience God's peace. Through daily prayer and Scripture reading, I have come to terms with the fact that God has a loving plan for my life and for the lives of my children. As the Word tells us, "In their hearts humans plan their course, but the LORD establishes their steps" (Proverbs 16:9 NIV).

The truth is that we will all find ourselves on paths that we don't want. And although we may pray with tearful desperation, God does not immediately—or sometimes ever—change that path.

While it might seem like devastating divine entrapment to be on a road we didn't choose, the sovereignty of God is meant to give us great peace while we travel it. This is because the God who is ultimately in control of the path our lives take is the same God who leads us—like the Israelites—from bondage to freedom. As we follow him, our souls can rest knowing that he has determined our life plan. And that plan, as guaranteed in Scripture, is always good (Romans 8:28).

Our souls can rest knowing that he has determined our life plan.

Like Moses, we may not want to walk forward into what is ahead, and we often won't know or understand all that we face. But just as Moses could not imagine the glory that was up ahead for him and his people, we cannot see all that is ahead in our own lives either. Take heart that the God who sees the end from the beginning is doing a good thing in and through you as you relent to his good and perfect will.

• **REFLECT:** Take a deep breath and remember that what may feel like divine entrapment is actually the path to freedom in God's plan. You don't have to figure it all out or understand it. God is at work. Take heart; there is glory up ahead!

_____

_____

_____

DAY 8

Peace in Choosing Obedience

*So Moses took his wife and his sons and had them ride
on a donkey, and went back to the land of Egypt.
And Moses took the staff of God in his hand.*

Exodus 4:20

● **Read Exodus 4:18–31** ●

The flame in the bush dissipated, and the air filled with emptiness where God's presence had been. Moses pressed knuckles into his eyes, shoving back the tears that threatened.

Everything had changed. And now he must change too.

Heaving a great sigh, Moses slipped the sandals back on his feet, each grain of sand a reminder that this was not a dream.

It was time to go to Egypt.

But first, he must request permission from his father-in-law to take his wife and his sons with him, away from their family home here in the desert.

He found Jethro in his tent, working the ledgers. Ducking under the tent flap, Moses cleared his throat and stood in front of his father-in-law.

"Moses! I thought you were with the flocks today, no?" Moses shook his head. Jethro crossed his arms and raised an eyebrow.

"I was, Father. But—" He stopped short. How to explain all that had happened? All that must change? It was a weight on his shoulders, in his very being.

Jethro must have felt the gravity too. He leaned back and uncrossed his arms. "What is it, Moses?"

He could not explain it all—did not even know if Jethro would believe him. "Please let me go back to my brothers in Egypt to see whether they are still alive."

Jethro stood up and closed the distance between them. He placed two strong hands on Moses' shoulders and looked him in the eye. "It's time for you to go, isn't it, son?"

Moses nodded, emotion thick in his throat. Jethro was a good man. He had welcomed him into his family so many years ago, when Moses had nothing to his name.

"Look at me, Moses." Jethro lifted one hand to Moses' head in blessing. "Go, Moses. Go in *peace*."

Has the Lord ever led you to do something you didn't want to do?

The last thing *I* wanted to do was knock on that door. My breathing shortened and my stomach roiled. I was afraid.

But I had to do this.

For weeks, the Lord had been impressing upon my heart the need to ask for forgiveness from a woman I'd known for nearly a decade but hadn't spoken with for years. As far as she knew, our relationship was fine, if cordial. But I had talked about her behind her back and disparaged her in front of others. She didn't know this—but the Lord did. My sin was plain before him, and he wasn't letting me off the hook.

I had repented to the Lord for my callous words and for my self-righteousness, hoping that would be the end of it. But as I continued to pray, the Lord brought verses to my mind multiple times—verses about trying to offer something to God while still being at odds with a brother: "First be reconciled to your brother, and then come and offer your gift" (see Matthew 5:23–24). The Lord was showing me that until I made this right, my relationship with him would be hindered because of my sin.

I was afraid. I didn't know how the conversation would go, and I feared being vulnerable with this woman—and facing the shame I would rightly feel when I told her the truth and saw the hurt in her eyes.

But God would not let me off the hook. I needed to obey him if I wanted to be free of this burden of sin. I needed to repent to this woman and ask for her forgiveness.

And that was why I was knocking on her door. I hadn't told her I was coming. I hadn't told anyone what I was doing. I had just shown up, compelled by the Holy Spirit and the Word of God.

When Moses found himself standing with his feet still bare in the desert sand, he could not yet rejoice in God's plan for his life, but he did relent to it. He surrendered. He obeyed and gave himself to the work that God had for him.

Here is the amazing thing that happens, though, when we relent to the Lord's path for us rather than the one we want for ourselves: We start to experience his peace. Our souls are able to be at rest in God even when our lives are full of pain and fear.

This transformation of soul is not usually immediate, but it *is* possible—just as we see in the life of Moses. For when he hears God speak to him out of the burning bush, he is fearful and panicked by what is ahead of him. And yet, as Moses follows the Lord, he is given the strength to do the next right thing. Even in his first step of obedience—asking his father-in-law for permission to take his family back to Egypt—the Scripture hints at the ultimate peace that is up ahead for him. Jethro, his father-in-law, responds to Moses' inquiry with a blessing: "Go in *peace*" (Exodus 4:18, emphasis added). The word *peace* here is the same Hebrew word that is commonly used in the Old Testament: *shalom*. The word has overtones of completeness, wholeness, and welfare. But it also connects to the idea of having peace with God in a covenant relationship.

> Our souls are able to be at rest in God even when our lives are full of pain and fear.

Moses, who has just felt the heat of God's presence and has heard the quake of God's voice, is being sent out in God's peace to go and do God's work.

Yes, Moses is afraid of facing his past. The path ahead is not an easy one for him. But here is true faith: He obeys anyway. His fear does not keep him from obedience.

That is what I had to do when I stood at that door to repent: choose obedience over fear. By the grace of God, I did it. I spoke the painful words of my sin toward this sister in Christ and told her the truth. I repented with sincerity and honesty; in God's kindness, she forgave me.

And after I left, what I felt was God's *peace*. I still had to wrestle with the repercussions of my sin in that relationship, but I had obeyed the Lord. My soul could again be at rest in God's presence, because I had obeyed him.

Most of us have areas in our life where we are afraid to obey God because we know the cost will be high. But to have fullness of peace with the Lord, we must obey him—both in the big things and in the seemingly small things. We will have to *choose* to obey God, turning our feet toward the thing that must be done and walking in that direction. Like Moses,

we must all walk toward our own Egypts—and trust that as we do, we will experience the same *shalom* that God blessed Moses with through Jethro.

• **REFLECT:** Where is God asking you to fully obey him right now? What choices do you need to make—today—to set your feet on the path of obedience? Ask God to help you do so, and trust that as you obey, you will experience his peace.

_____

_____

_____

DAY 9

Peace When Obedience Makes Things Worse

Then Moses turned to the Lord and said, "O Lord, why have you done evil to this people? Why did you ever send me? For since I came to Pharaoh to speak in your name, he has done evil to this people, and you have not delivered your people at all."

Exodus 5:22–23

• **Read Exodus 5:1–23** •

Moses tried to straighten his knees into submission, but they shook like branches in the wind. He was thankful for his robe and how it hid his fear. But he could not be thankful for his voice. It shook too—and there would be no hiding it. Perhaps Aaron would have to take over.

There, before the throne of the most powerful man in the world—his brother, Pharaoh, king of Egypt—Moses spoke the words God had given to him: "Thus says the Lord, the God of Israel, 'Let my people go, that they may hold a feast to me in the wilderness'" (Exodus 5:1).

His brother glared at him. "Who are 'your people,' Moses? I thought I was, wasn't I?" He flicked his wrist, and a servant offered him a drink—of what, Moses couldn't see. Pharaoh was baiting him, waiting for him to speak and break the awkward silence that hung like a cloak around the entire throne room. It was a game Pharaoh had played with Moses his whole life—knowing how he hated to speak, forcing him to do it at inopportune times.

But this was not a game.

Moses kept his eyes straight ahead and his mouth shut. He would not be baited; he had said what God told him to say.

After a long pull on his goblet, Pharaoh smashed it to the floor. Moses couldn't help it; he jumped.

"Who is the Lord, that I should obey his voice and let Israel go? I do not know the Lord, and I will not let Israel go." Pharaoh's bellow ricocheted off the walls.

Moses glowered at the brother he had once had.

Aaron spoke now. "God has met with us. Please let us go sacrifice to him, lest he discipline us with sickness or war!"

Pharaoh sneered. "You do not need to meet with this so-called 'god.' Your people need to *work*." He dismissed them with a flick of his wrist.

Later in the day, murmurs of anger and disbelief flitted through the camp. Pharaoh had determined that the Israelites should go and gather the straw they needed for brickmaking; before, the straw had been provided. They still had to make the same number of bricks each day, but their work had just gotten much, *much* harder.

Moses felt a sob rise in his throat. What had they done?

※

Sometimes, obedience to God seems to make things worse.

Before Michael worked at a bank, and before he became a pastor, he worked in financial services in the Chicago area. He had started a new, completely commission-based position in the months right before the Great Recession. If we had known what was ahead, he wouldn't have signed on for a sales job prior to a huge financial downturn. But, of course, we couldn't know.

What I *did* know was that it was going to be a step of faith for us to take a job without any guaranteed income, and I was more than a little nervous about it. Still, Michael had the skills and personality to do this job well. We had prayed about him taking the job and felt like this was the Lord's will for us. In the big game of risk versus reward, we took as much risk out of the equation as we could.

But then the economy plummeted.

It wasn't uncommon for Michael to work twelve- to fourteen-hour days before coming home to lead a small group with me and then collapsing into bed. A year into this job, no matter how hard he worked, it wasn't getting any better.

I remember the frustration I felt toward the Lord: Here we were, doing our best, just trying to obey him. I was working two part-time jobs, we were leading a small group at church, and we were volunteering additional hours on Sundays every week. Weren't we being obedient? Weren't we trying to follow God?

As the recession wore on, it got worse and worse, and no wonder: When people aren't making money, they don't have any to save or invest.

We pulled money out of our savings to plug the gaps in our budget. We cut out everything we could think of that we didn't need. Michael took peanut butter and jelly sandwiches to work as his colleagues ate out. We overdrew on our bank account for the first time.

It felt like our obedience to the Lord in taking this job was being met with more struggle, and I couldn't understand it.

When Pharaoh increased the Israelites' physical labor, the Israelites were furious with Moses. They railed against him, yelling that he had "put a sword in [the hands of Pharaoh and his servants] to kill us!" (Exodus 5:21). Moses now feared Pharaoh *and* his own people—and he also feared that God would not fulfill his promise. He cried out to the Lord in distress: "Why did you ever send me? For since I came to Pharaoh to speak in your name, he has done evil to this people, and you have not delivered your people at all" (Exodus 5:22–23). We can hear the desperation in his words—and his confusion as well: Moses was obeying God, but his life was getting worse! His own people hated him, their lives were harder because of him, and the Lord hadn't delivered them yet.

Perhaps you have felt this way too. You are faithfully obeying God, and yet your life appears to be on a downward spiral. Things go from bad to worse. God's work in your life seems minimal—or perhaps nonexistent. People you trust turn against you. Life gets even harder. Your faith feels weak and small. You doubt your Lord and yourself.

You are afraid.

This is where Moses was—afraid of his own people, and afraid that God would fail to fulfill his word.

Even when the Lord responds to his fear and declares that deliverance is assured, Moses is still disbelieving: "Behold, the people of Israel have not listened to me. How then shall Pharaoh listen to me, for I am of uncircumcised lips?" (Exodus 6:12).

Moses is wavering in his belief. His obedience has gotten him nothing but trouble. He isn't sure if God will do what he has promised. He lacks faith. He lacks peace.

And yet, as he continues to obey the Lord—even in his fear—we see Moses' peace and confidence grow.

Obediently, Moses goes back to Pharaoh and declares the word of the Lord to him—words full of plague and destruction. And then? With every plague that God demonstrates against Egypt, Moses sees God fulfilling his promises.

God shows himself faithful as Moses continues to obey. The breakthrough is not immediate, but over time.

Often our lives look this way as well: Immediate obedience to God brings rejection, or cultural ostracism, or hardship, or trial. We are considered weird or radical by others for believing the Word of God and following it. Like Moses, we may even face anger from our own family or community!

But as Moses endures in his obedience to the Lord, he sees the Lord make good on his word. It doesn't happen all at once; instead, it was *obedience over time* that led to Moses' faith growing—and to the deliverance of his people.

—※—

When we followed God into Michael's commission-based job, it led to strain, anxiety, and frustration. The economy went from bad to worse; our struggles increased. But in ways we couldn't yet see, it also led to Michael's entrance into ministry—because less than a year after he quit that job, Michael became a pastor on staff at a church. We kept obeying God into the next thing, and it led to great peace as we discovered what we were created to do: minister to God's people through the local church.

> Obedience to Christ often leads to short-term trial but produces long-term glory.

If you are in a situation today where you have been obeying God and things are challenging and difficult, take heart and be at peace. Obedience does not always—or even often—bring about immediate breakthrough or peace. Instead, obedience to Christ usually leads to short-term trial that produces long-term glory: "And after you have suffered a little while, the God of all grace, who has called you to his eternal glory in Christ, will himself restore, confirm, strengthen, and establish you" (1 Peter 5:10).

• **REFLECT:** Where does obedience to Christ feel hard right now? Ask him for the strength to persevere and the peace that you need to keep putting one foot in front of the other.

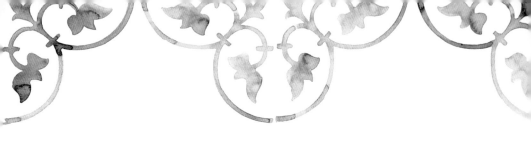

DAY 10

Finding Confident Peace in God

*"Fear not, stand firm, and see the salvation of the Lord,
which he will work for you today. For the Egyptians whom
you see today, you shall never see again. The Lord will fight
for you, and you have only to be silent."*

Exodus 14:13–14

• **Read Exodus 14:10-31** •

M oses could hear the thundering of thousands of hooves racing toward them in the dark. Pharaoh and his army were coming. The Lord had told him they would.

There were over a million of them—God's people—here at the edge of the Red Sea. But the hooves and the yells from the Egyptian army made the waves sound like raindrops.

Panic was in the air; the people were screaming at him now, yelling on every side. A burly man on his right: "Is it because there are no graves in Egypt that you have taken us away to die in the wilderness?" The mother in front of him, holding a screaming child to her chest: "Is not this what we said to you in Egypt: 'Leave us alone that we may serve the Egyptians'? Better than to die in the wilderness!"

Fear rippled around him in a groundswell, but Moses' heart was steady. He knew that God was going to come through. How? The Lord had not told him, but he believed they would be delivered.

He turned around and spoke to the multitudes, his voice carrying like thunder: "Fear not, stand firm, and see the salvation of the Lord, which he will work for you today. For the Egyptians whom you see today, you shall never see again. The Lord will fight for you, and you have only to be silent" (Exodus 14:13-14).

And then that voice—the same one that had startled and scared him in the burning bush so many months ago—spoke to him.

"Tell the people of Israel to go forward. Lift up your staff, and stretch out your hand over the sea and divide it, that the people of Israel may go through the sea on dry ground. And I will harden the hearts of the Egyptians so that they shall go in after them, and I will get glory over Pharaoh and all his host, his chariots, and his horsemen. And the Egyptians shall know that I am the Lord, when I have gotten glory over Pharaoh, his chariots, and his horsemen" (Exodus 14:15-18).

In the same moment, the pillar of God's presence with them moved behind the Israelites and shielded them from the approaching army. The people stilled and looked to him.

Moses lifted up his staff across the sea and watched with ever-increasing wonder as walls of water formed in front of him, slowly at first, and then with a mighty blast. There was sand between those watery walls—a pathway to freedom.

Moses' face was a sheen of tears. "You are the Lord! And we, your people, will follow you!"

⸝

Who is this man? This confident leader at the front of God's people? Moses is a man who has seen God's hand at work.

Through the plagues against Egypt, God proves his power to Pharaoh and to the Israelites—and to Moses—again and again. By the time the Israelites have lived through the Passover and have victoriously left Egypt, Moses is a man full of peace and confidence in God. In fact, his faith in God's sovereignty and power is so certain that when Pharaoh's army corners the Israelites up against the Red Sea, Moses responds to the people with unwavering assurance.

This is a pivotal moment for Moses.

Before, when the Israelites had questioned and berated Moses in Egypt, his fear of them had him crying to God in distress. But now, as the people again scream against Moses, his response to the people's tirade is quick and sure: *Fear not! Stand firm!* Moses has no fear and speaks that same assurance to them.

What has changed? How has Moses transformed?

Moses knows the Lord.

That is what has changed everything for him.

When he met God in the burning bush, Moses did not yet know the great I AM. He had no history with him, no personal experience of God's power. But now, at the edge of the Red Sea, Moses knows the Lord. He has seen God fulfill his word over and over again through each miraculous plague that descended upon Egypt. He has experienced the grace of the first Passover and has seen over a million slaves freed from Pharaoh's grasp. He and his people are already living in a miracle, and he knows that God will finish what he has started. He will fulfill his word. They *will* be delivered.

Moses has confidence that God will fulfill his promises for his people because of who God is, not because of what Moses can see or understand.

And so, here on the edge of impossibility, Moses no longer fears that God will not come through. Instead, he declares to the Israelites that God will fight for them *before* he knows how God will do it. Moses' soul is at rest because he trusts that God will fulfill his promise to his people.

He is a man at peace, even when he is stuck between an army and an ocean.

In the months following Michael's firing, my anxieties and worries about the future threatened to overwhelm me, and I became desperate for peace—hungry for it as I had never been before. In that desperation, the Lord impressed upon my heart that peace—if I was to experience it—would have to be found right where I was. Our circumstances were not guaranteed to change.

God was inviting me, afresh, to find my peace in him.

I read the Bible with a heart hungry to see God providing for his people, and Moses' life fit the bill. Searching through the Scriptures, I was stunned once again by the parting of the Red Sea and how the Lord tangibly provided a new path for his people to freedom—a path where there had never been one before. I marveled at how God led Moses from a man of wavering fear to a confident and peaceful leader. And I was challenged to respond like him, trusting that God would fulfill his promises for our family because of who he is, not because of what I could see or understand.

> God will fulfill his promise for me because of who he is, not because of what I can understand.

As I read the Word and steeped myself in the stories of Scripture, my faith in God began to grow stronger than my fear. The experiences of so many saints in the Bible strengthened my belief that the same God who made a way for the Israelites would make a way for us. The same Lord who gave food to the hungry and provided breakthrough in impossible circumstances would provide for us.

Still, nothing changed.

Except that everything did—inside of me. I started to experience God's peace in the midst of that unchanging season for our family. The more I read the Word, the more I came to know God. And the more I came to know him, the more I came to see and trust that God had a loving plan for my life, Michael's life, and the lives of our children. I clung to the truth that our lives were mapped out by the Lord and our steps were already established by him (Proverbs 16:9). God was in control of our lives.

When we were nearly five months out from Michael's job loss, I had the realization that I was no longer looking inwardly at my fear but, instead, I was looking outward at Christ. The Word of God had chipped away at my anxieties and replaced it with the Lord's peace.

This is the peace in Christ that is available to us. While we may not be called to lead God's people through the Red Sea, we have been given the opportunity to walk in faith rather than in fear, and to experience God's peace even when our lives feel stuck in impossible situations.

Take your anxieties and fears to the Word of God today. Read the stories of Moses, of Sarah, of Ruth, and of Jesus, and take them to heart. Remember all that he has done for you already, and praise him that he always is and always has been at work for his people.

He will deliver you.

You are never alone.

Be at peace.

- **REFLECT:** Dive in to God's Word today—reread the story of Moses if you need some encouragement! In the midst of whatever you face today, God is your Deliverer, and his peace is available to you even in the middle of impossible situations!

RUTH

Peace in Financial Distress

DAYS 11–15

DAY 11

Peace When You Lose It All

So [Naomi] set out from the place where she was with
her two daughters-in-law, and they went on the way
to return to the land of Judah.

Ruth 1:7

• **Read Ruth 1:1–7** •

The moan that bubbled up from deep in her chest threatened to undo her, but Ruth would not let it come out. *I cannot break down now, not again. Just one foot in front of the other. Just keep moving.* She willed her body to move through the sludge of sorrow that felt like thick mud up to her knees.

The past week had been the worst of her life; she had not imagined it could get any worse after the year they had just gone through.

Ruth had lived with her husband and in-laws in Moab, all of them content, all of them yearning for the pitter-patter of little feet in the home. Although widowed, her mother-in-law, Naomi, was the happy matriarch of their little clan. But the famine that had dragged on for years had stretched them past the edge of comfort and into the pain of hunger. When her brother-in-law had dropped dead in the field seven months ago, her precious sister-in-law, Orpah, had nearly died with him, weeping daily for the last half year. Ruth could not blame her; losing a husband was usually the assurance of poverty. But Mahlon had generously taken on the burden of caring for Orpah too.

Mahlon: Ruth's own husband. He was a kind man—not overly emotional or effusive with praise, but a good man. And she loved him. Still, with one man and three women in their small family, money had been tight but manageable if they ate little, which they did.

Now Mahlon was gone too. A week ago to this very day, he had caught a fever. Within three days, he was unresponsive. Two days ago, all breath had left his lungs.

It was too much to bear.

Just keep walking. Don't think about the past. Ruth trudged on.

Naomi had packed up their few belongings this morning, hours after Mahlon's burial. She said she was going back to her homeland—to Bethlehem, where there were rumors of food. Ruth was following her; what else could she do?

It felt like everything she loved was gone, evaporated like mist on a summer morning. Moab, too, was a dry husk, all life from the land ripped out through too much heat. There was no food that could grow. Her husband was dead, and her womb was empty. She was a young widow with no dowry; her family had long since turned her aside when she married a foreigner. She had no money, no prospects, no hope.

What would she do? *Just put one foot in front of the other.*

—※—

I looked at our budget again and ran a hand down my face. "So we're both quitting our jobs?" Michael was piling dishes into the dishwasher. "Yep."

"With nothing lined up in St. Louis?"

The clink of glass came from the kitchen as he found an open spot for the last bowls. "Correct."

I sighed and tried to ignore the churning in my gut, then chuckled aloud. "Right. Sounds like a plan."

We were either faithful or crazy—I was hoping faithful. After several years on staff at a church in the Chicago area, Michael and I both believed he needed to go to seminary full time. Down the line, he wanted to become a lead pastor, and we knew a seminary degree would be necessary. He had been taking a class or two each semester alongside of his pastoral position, but with a new baby and the pressures of ministry, the pace at which we were living wasn't sustainable.

We were exhausted.

The more we prayed, the more we felt like it was time for him to become a full-time seminarian at a school in St. Louis—four hours and a new state away.

When Michael got accepted into the program, I quit my job as a college English instructor and Michael left his pastoral position; we were giving up both of our incomes in order for him to go back to school. I can imagine that from the outside, our choices looked foolish. But we both believed that this was the faithful decision for our family long-term, even if it made things more difficult in the short-term.

A big piece of the puzzle before we moved, however, was selling our condo in the Chicago suburbs. According to the bylaws of the homeowners' association, we were not allowed to rent it out—we had to sell. Making some money on the sale would help us stay afloat for the coming months in seminary.

But the housing market in our area tanked. After months of being on the market, and over thirty showings later, we finally ended up selling our condo for $40,000 less than we had purchased it for six years beforehand. We were a handbreadth away from being under water.

I remember feeling so defeated: We were going to seminary to serve the Lord! Shouldn't this be easier? Was this really what faithfulness looked like for us? Maybe we *were* foolish. We were heading to a new city with a toddler, no jobs, and the need to figure out how to pay for the basics like housing, food, diapers, and clothes.

We didn't know what to do but move forward and trust the Lord, trying the best we could to follow him.

When Ruth found herself a young widow in Moab, she was stripped bare. As a woman in an ancient culture, she had little to no rights, no way (at least no moral way) to make money, and apparently she had no one to fall back on, since the other men in her borrowed family were dead. Imagine the fear and anxiety that Ruth faced as a woman in a precarious position—on top of an already unstable national situation with the ongoing famine. Position, power, money, and cultural security were all lost to her: Women without men to protect them were at risk of danger and disuse. She did not even have the boon of a child in her womb to bring the hope of income someday—if it was a son. No, Ruth was destitute. She had nothing in front of her. I can imagine that her soul was far from being at rest. There were countless worries to face; she had lost all she ever had.

Perhaps you find yourself today like Ruth, facing the anxieties and grief of loss and financial strain. Or perhaps you feel more like I did when I wrestled with the fear of not knowing how we were going to start over financially in a new set of circumstances. Maybe your story is different altogether. But no

> Often, peace is found in the simplest—and hardest—kind of obedience: walking with Christ.

matter where we find ourselves today, all of us know what it's like to be worried about finances to some degree.

For many of us, the fear of financial instability is intimately tied to the loss of security.

This is what Ruth experienced after the death of her husband. All she had was gone, and with it, any security or consistency in her life. Still, the Scriptures point us to a woman who, though understandably emotional, is still ultimately responsive to God's plan.

She could have refused to move forward in life. Her fear and grief could have stopped her. Instead, she followed Naomi on the long road out of Moab. Why? Perhaps Ruth was seeking the peace that existed when she followed the Lord. Did she know where the road with Naomi would lead, practically or spiritually? Hardly. But Ruth *did* know that Naomi followed the one true God. If Ruth wanted to follow Yahweh, she had to follow Naomi.

And so she did.

On a smaller scale, this is what our little family tried to do as well. When we left for St. Louis with no assurance that what was ahead would work out, we were trying to follow the Lord Jesus. We kept doing the next thing to obey him, even if it looked foolish from the outside. We didn't know how we would pay the bills or if we would have enough in the coming months, but both of us felt the inexplicable peace that comes from walking in step with our Good Shepherd.

So keep walking with him. Often, peace is found in the simplest—and hardest—kind of obedience: continuing to choose Christ and walk in step with him even when the world falls apart around us.

- **REFLECT:** Today, seek to focus on Christ rather than on any financial strain or difficult circumstances. Yes, this is hard. Sometimes it feels nearly impossible. Meditate on Proverbs 3:5–6 and keep putting one foot in front of the other, choosing to walk with Jesus.

DAY 12

Peace in Following God
into Uncertainty

*"For where you go I will go, and where you lodge I will lodge.
Your people shall be my people, and your God my God."*

Ruth 1:16

• **Read Ruth 1:8–22** •

They were nearing the border of Moab when Naomi turned around to face Ruth and Orpah, who had been shuffling alongside her within a cloud of her own grief.

"Go, return each of you to her mother's house." She placed a hand on each of their heads. "May the Lord deal kindly with you, as you have dealt with the dead and with me."

Ruth could not help it; the unbidden tears washed like a flood down her face. Both she and Orpah said the same: They would go with her to Bethlehem.

Naomi deterred them with her many reasons: She was too old to marry again and bear sons that her daughters-in-law could then marry. They needed husbands, and she had no way to give them what they needed. Naomi's face turned to flint. "No, my daughters, for it is exceedingly bitter to me for your sake that the hand of the Lord has gone out against me. Turn back."

All three of them cried on the road together, knowing the truth of her words and her pain. The sun blazed against Ruth's shoulders like heat from an open fire, and her mind whirled like a bird in a cage. *What should I do?*

Orpah untangled herself from the other two women and, without speaking, kissed Ruth and then Naomi. With puffy eyes, she turned back to Moab and started the long road to her mother's house.

Ruth reflected on the love and care she had known from the hand of this woman. Naomi was more a mother to her than her own, and the ways of the Israelites had become her ways too—because Naomi had taught her. There might be no future for her with Naomi; she could not be sure. But she would not go back to Moab.

Like a rod through her spine, the decision shot through Ruth. She made her choice, knelt, and wrapped her arms around Naomi's knees.

Naomi tried to pull her off. "Orpah has gone back to her people and to her gods; return after her!"

Ruth shook her head and clung tighter. "Do not urge me to leave you, Mother. For where you go I will go, and where you lodge I will lodge. Your people shall be my people, and your God my God. Where you die, I will die, and there will I be buried." She released a breath and made a solemn vow. "May the Lord do so to me and more also if anything but death parts me from you."

Naomi's eyes glistened with tears, and although she did not say a word, she took Ruth's hand. They walked forward to Bethlehem together.

Michael started seminary in St. Louis, and I kept looking for a job that would pay the bills. Teaching positions at Christian colleges were rare, and it wouldn't work for me to take a job where I had to pay more for childcare than what I would be making.

We had about two or three months left where we could squeak by financially, and then things were going to be difficult.

As we prayed about the right job for me, I couldn't shake the thought of starting my own business. I had loved teaching writers as a college instructor and wondered if there was a way to continue teaching if it wasn't through a university. As an academic, that was the path that I knew and understood: Go to school for a million years and then teach in higher education. I had done that, and I had thoroughly enjoyed it; in many ways, teaching college students was a sweet spot for me. But I had also taught a few writing classes through an online ministry, and women had signed up in droves. It gave me the idea of teaching writing classes online—not through a university or another ministry, but by creating my own company. I could teach Christ-centered writing classes to women across the country (and even the world)!

I hesitated; I'd never thought of myself as an entrepreneur. I had followed the path set before me with school and landed as an academic, not a businesswoman. Besides, the risk seemed like it could be greater than the reward. What if I did everything to create a company and it was a complete flop? What if no one wanted to take the classes I offered?

I ran the numbers and determined that I would need a thousand dollars to get started, for everything from a website designer and a logo to website hosting and professional photos. For most businesses, that wouldn't be much of a start-up cost. But for us as a seminary family, it felt huge.

But other options were slim, and it felt like starting Writing with Grace—the name for my new venture—was what the Lord was leading me to. I sensed his direction and peace every time I prayed about it, and so did Michael. It seemed like the Lord was asking me to walk forward with him into an uncertain circumstance financially and practically. This was an opportunity for me to obey him and trust him in a new way.

I was scared that it would be a complete failure, that *I* would be a failure. And what then? What if this business failed before it even started? How would our family make it?

—✳—

When Ruth took Naomi's hand on the road out of Moab, she had no idea what was ahead. They were destitute women in a culture that valued rich men. They had no home, no family, no opportunity. Theirs was an awful circumstance.

It was exceedingly hard for these two women. In fact, when they finally got to Naomi's hometown of Bethlehem, Naomi was so distraught that she declared to the townswomen that she had changed her name from "pleasantness" to Mara, which means "bitter": "The Almighty has made my life very bitter. I went away full, but the LORD has brought me back empty. Why call me Naomi? The LORD has afflicted me; the Almighty has brought misfortune upon me" (Ruth 1:20–21 NIV). Naomi was now declaring to the whole town that she was bitter, empty, afflicted, and full of misfortunes.

It would not have been a happy arrival to their new home.

And while it might seem that Ruth's silence in the Scripture is because she is overwhelmed, or afraid, or worried, I don't think that's the case. Surely she felt these emotions to some degree, but as the book of Ruth unfolds, we find a woman who is anything but afraid. She is bold and assured in her actions. She is a woman at peace in the hardest of circumstances.

Why? Because Ruth was not just following Naomi; she was ultimately following God. Financially and practically, her life was in ruin. But she had walked *with God* into this new situation. Her pledge to her mother-in-law was not only a pledge to be with Naomi—it was a pledge to follow the Lord: "Your people shall be my people, and your God my God" (Ruth 1:16).

Their circumstances were hard beyond imagining: so much loss, so little hope. But even when Naomi declared her bitterness and frustration, Ruth did not go back on her promise. She stayed with Naomi and Naomi's God—the Lord—because she believed that it was worth it to follow him into uncertainty rather than go back to a life without him. That is where Ruth's peace and confidence came from: knowing that walking with God into uncertainty was better than any type of security without him.

> It is worth it to follow God into uncertainty rather than live without him.

Jesus will sometimes call us to follow him into uncertain circumstances—financially or practically—that don't have any clear outcome. We want to be wise in how we live (see Matthew 10:16), but we cannot get around the fact that God often asks his people to follow him into circumstances that are anything *but* secure by the world's standards.

Yet true security comes from Christ alone and from knowing that our future in him is eternally secure because of the victory he won for us over death and sin on the cross (see 1 Peter 1:3–5). With that in mind, we can be at peace even in situations as difficult as Ruth and Naomi's, because we know that he cares for us.

- **REFLECT:** Whatever your circumstance today, take heart. You don't have to know what is ahead, financially or practically, in order to have peace in Christ. If you're walking with him and obeying him to the best of your ability, he will guide you. So how can you take a step of obedience today? Ask the Lord for the strength to obey him, and trust that he will meet you in your obedience.

DAY 13

The Peace of Being in Need

"May you be richly rewarded by the Lord, the God of Israel, under whose wings you have come to take refuge."

Ruth 2:12 NIV

• **Read Ruth 2:1–23** •

Ruth looked at the road in front of her. *Left or right?* Both held fields that she could glean in.

A breath of wind, gentle as a caress, turned her head to the left, and she felt a peace cover her from head to toe. *Is this how the Lord speaks to his children?*

The field was being harvested not far down the road. Rolling up her sleeves, Ruth fell in line as far behind the women workers as she could, picking up the broken pieces of grain that the harvesters had left.

Within an hour, she had sweat through her clothes. The sun was at its peak, and her grief mingled with her physical exhaustion, drawing tears from her eyes. *God of Israel, help me.*

The crunch of rock turned her gaze upward to a man walking toward her, carrying authority with him. Her stomach tumbled. Had she done something wrong?

He was still far off. "My daughter!" Ruth looked behind her, but there was no one else around. The man smiled as he stopped. "Please, listen to me. Don't go and glean in anyone else's field. Stay here with the women who work for me." He nodded his head toward the men up ahead. "I have told the men not to lay a hand on you." He studied her, and Ruth found that her tongue refused to work. His eyebrows shot up. "Are you thirsty? Feel free to go and get a drink from the water jars at any time."

Ruth dropped to her knees, overcome by his kindness. In this new city, as a foreigner with no husband and no way to make money, she had assumed she would always be an outcast. She bowed her face to the dirt and found her voice through her tears: "Why have I found such favor in your eyes that you notice me—a foreigner?"

The man's voice gentled. "I've been told all about what you have done for your mother-in-law since the death of your husband—how you left your father and mother and your homeland and came to live with a people you didn't know. May the Lord repay you for what you have done." When she looked up at him with shock, he laughed and spread his arms to the heavens. "May you be richly rewarded by the Lord, the God of Israel, under whose wings you have come to take refuge!"

In need.

That's how I felt, and it made me uncomfortable. In need. Needy.

As I did the work to get my business idea off the ground, life still went on. Our daughter, Ella, was three years old and had recurrent croup—a condition that was both scary and expensive, as it required a lot of doctor's visits, night trips to the emergency department, and even, occasionally, ambulance rides. The awful air quality in St. Louis heightened her croup to the worst levels she'd ever had, and I didn't know how we'd manage the medical bills. She was sick and I was scared. Of course, we would get her whatever help she needed—but in the process, I was afraid we were going to dig ourselves into a financial hole.

I talked to Ella's new pediatrician to ask if they had any medical discount we could apply for. He recommended that we check to see if Ella was eligible for Medicaid. If she was, all of her medical care would be paid for by the state of Missouri.

All of it.

As the daughter of a physician, I was used to having good medical coverage and lots of options. Now, as an adult with my own child, the situation was different. The medical insurance we could afford in St. Louis didn't offer many options and only covered catastrophic situations. But I'd never considered applying for medical benefits through the state; I didn't see myself as someone "in need," or view us as a family that required help to pay our own bills. Surely we could work harder or figure out a way to pay for things ourselves.

But our financial realities made me face my pride: we *were* in need. Ella required solid and consistent medical care that far outstripped our ability to pay for it. We couldn't provide for our daughter on our own.

We needed help.

As uneasy as I felt about getting help from the state, I also sensed the Lord was doing something in me that went deeper than medical bills. He was knocking down my false vision of provision and of thinking that Michael and I were our own providers. He was tearing down my desire to do it all on my own. *"Let me care for you,"* I felt like he was saying. *"See my hand in this provision, even if it's not what you expected or wanted."*

When Ruth started gleaning in Boaz's field, what she expected was probably to be ignored (and possibly even treated badly). She was doing the work of picking up the leftovers in the field—the bits of food reserved for the "poor and the foreigner," according to God's law (see Leviticus 19:9–10 NIV). Gleaning was the equivalent of an Israelite handout.

It took humility—a lowliness of spirit and an admission that she needed help—for Ruth to glean in the fields. And she was willing to take that road. In fact, when she went with Naomi to Bethlehem, she might have even expected it. What were their other options?

What she didn't expect was the kindness and favor she received from Boaz. He offered her protection and provision; the Scriptures tell us that she left the fields that first day lugging nearly thirty pounds of grain! Can you imagine the peace and confidence Ruth had as she walked home to Naomi? She could continue to glean there, protected and provided for as long as the harvest went on. For a destitute woman with two mouths to feed, this gift of kindness was miraculous.

—⚹—

In our need, most of us do not expect to be met with kindness and favor. The culture that we live in tells us to work harder and make our own way in the world—to provide for ourselves and never expect a free lunch. And while the Bible is clear about working diligently and being excellent in all that we do (see Colossians 3:23), the truth is that none of us really make our own way in the world. Every talent and ability that we have been given comes from God and is meant to ultimately go back to God in praise (see 1 Peter 4:10–11).

Putting Ella on Medicaid was a small picture of this reality for me; we couldn't make our own way when it came to caring for her. I expected to have to work harder and try to figure out how to pay for our daughter's care on our own, because I didn't think we needed help. But as the medical bills piled up, God used the enormity of our need to lovingly push me to acknowledge how much help we *actually* needed (newsflash: it was a lot).

The amazing thing? Once we asked for help, it was granted: Ella's medical care was covered for the eighteen months we lived in St. Louis. It was an immense grace to our family, and one that filled me with peace as I experienced God providing for us.

All of us will face seasons of being in need, financially or otherwise. But far past our need for practical provision, we must all come face-to-face with our truest reality of being a people who are desperately in need of God's grace.

Ruth needed God's grace as she went to glean. Our family needed his grace with our medical bills. And all of us need God's grace, today and for eternity; none of us can make our own way into heaven. We need the favor of God through the sacrifice and resurrection of Christ in order to attain the miraculous gift of salvation and eternal life in him!

And all of us need God's grace, today and for eternity.

Boaz was a picture of this grace to Ruth in the fields, offering her the peace of provision and protection. And today—even now—God is offering that same peace of his eternal provision and protection to you through faith in Christ.

- **REFLECT:** Have you accepted Christ's eternal gift of provision and protection through repenting of your sins and believing in him for your salvation? If you haven't, take time today to read these verses from the book of Romans: Romans 3:10, 23; 5:8, 12; 6:23; and 10:9-10. The gift of salvation is available to you today!

If you have already accepted the gift of salvation through Christ, thank the Lord for how he has cared for you and provided for you every day of your life up until now.

DAY 14

Peace When It's Out of Our Hands

*"I am Ruth, your servant. Spread your wings
over your servant, for you are a redeemer."*

Ruth 3:9

• **Read Ruth 3:1–13** •

Ruth shivered. She wasn't cold, but her nerves were getting the better of her.
If Naomi's plan didn't work, she would be disgraced. *Lord God, guide me.*

After a night of celebrating the harvest, Boaz had fallen asleep on the
threshing floor near the end of a pile of grain. There were other men on the
floor, but his strong frame was easy for Ruth to make out, even in the hazy
moonlight. She had seen him nearly every day for weeks, and his presence
had become a comfort to her.

Ruth tiptoed through the field until she could see his chest rise and fall
with the cadence of a man contented and dreaming, and she found herself
smiling at him in spite of her jitters. She looked around before walking
closer. Every man on the threshing floor had drunk enough wine to keep
them asleep for many hours.

Was Naomi crazy to tell her to do this? She had instructed Ruth to uncover Boaz's feet and lie down to wait for him to tell her what to do. And so that's what Ruth did, in the dark, holding her breath as she slid up against Boaz's feet, the small of her back under his toes.

She replayed the conversation she'd had with Naomi that morning in her mind: *"I want a husband for you, Ruth. And Boaz would make a good one."*

"Mother! He is a rich landowner; I am but a humble gleaner." Still, the fire that bloomed in Ruth's cheeks revealed her true feelings for the man.

Naomi laughed—the first real laugh Ruth had heard from her in months. *"I have seen you two together, Ruth. He cares for you; he would gladly take you as his bride. Besides, is he not our relative? He and Elimelech come from the same family tree. It is his right to claim you as the kinsman-redeemer of this family."*

Ruth snapped back to the present as she felt Boaz stir. She held her breath. *What is going to happen?* Naomi had explained that Boaz had the opportunity (if not the responsibility) to marry into their family so as to carry on the family name. Naomi was too old to have children, but Ruth—now part of Elimelech's line through marriage—could be redeemed by Boaz and made his wife.

And so Ruth was here, in the dark, at his feet. Her actions tonight—brash though they were—had been orchestrated by Naomi to push things to a point of decision. In essence, Ruth's presence here tonight was a request for Boaz to fulfill his responsibility to marry her. And if he rejected her—or worse, used her here tonight? Her reputation could be ruined forever.

The moon was at its zenith when Boaz woke with a start. His voice, usually clear and commanding, was unsettled in the dark.

His whisper was hoarse. "Who are you?"

Ruth spoke with more confidence than she really had, making sure to keep her voice low. "I am Ruth, your servant. Spread your wings over your servant, for you are a redeemer."

Boaz sat up and found her face in the dark. The tenderness she found there took her breath away.

He sighed deep and long. "May you be blessed by the Lord, my daughter. Your kindness is clear: You haven't gone after younger men, even when you could have."

She shook her head. Why would she? She had never met a man like Boaz. He reached down to spread his garment over her.

"Don't fear, my Ruth. I will do what you ask, with joy in my heart." She could see his soft smile in the moonlight. "The townsmen know what a worthy woman you are. And I *am* a redeemer to you." He paused, and she could not read his face. "But there is one redeemer nearer in kin than I. Stay here until the sun comes up, and then, in the morning, I will talk with him. If he will redeem you, he has the right to do so. But if not, as the Lord lives, *I* will redeem you."

Ruth's heart beat like a drum in her chest. She was going to be redeemed—married and cared for! But by whom? There was another man who could redeem her—a man she didn't know. A shiver raced down her back.

She rolled over in the dark. The path ahead was unclear.

Oh, God of the Israelites, let it be Boaz.

The day had come. I hadn't gotten a new job in St. Louis; instead, we had spent the thousand dollars it took to get Writing with Grace off the ground, and today was launch day for my entrepreneurial dream. I'm sure that many small business owners have lots of big feelings on the first day they open their doors or land their first client; the overriding emotions that I felt were excitement and fear.

I was truly afraid that the whole endeavor was going to tank—that no one would sign up for my first writing course, and that the time and effort I'd put into this would have been better spent searching for a new job.

Instead, I had taken three months to get Writing with Grace going: the same three months in reserve money we had in our bank account. Today was the moment of truth. If launch day (and launch week!) went poorly, our family was going to be stretched thin.

I had wrestled with feeling like a fool over those three months, wondering if this was one of the dumbest things I'd ever considered. But the peace that I felt as I continued to pray about Writing with Grace was consistent. I couldn't nail the emotion to the wall once and for all; I still felt waves of anxiety when I looked at our dwindling bank account. But my soul was at rest doing this work. My husband was peaceful, and my family and our close friends all thought I should go for it. I knew that I was trying to be faithful. And I also knew that if my little dream of Writing with Grace was a complete failure, at least it had been a failure based on faith and the counsel of my Christian community.

Now it was launch day: the day when the virtual doors opened for Writing with Grace. Would anyone sign up? I'd spent about a hundred dollars in marketing money on a few virtual ads and some business cards I'd handed out at a women's conference. Everything else would be word of mouth.

It was out of my hands.

—※—

So much of Ruth's life was completely out of her control. She was a foreigner in a foreign land, without power or prestige, at the mercy of Boaz and his workers for her daily bread. And when she followed Naomi's advice to nudge Boaz into marriage, she found the path of her life in the hands of her kinsman-redeemer. Would Boaz redeem her and marry her? Or would the other relative—a man she did not know—redeem and marry her instead? Her life and future are now at a critical turning point, and Ruth has no power to make anything happen. All she can do is go home with Naomi and wait.

She is completely dependent upon others.
She is completely dependent upon the Lord.

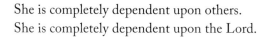

All of us have found ourselves in situations and seasons when life feels completely out of our control. When sickness or loss or financial strain come knocking on our doors, we often realize—with painful clarity—how little we have control over. When our bodies break down; when our bank account runs dry; when our families fall apart; when someone we love is lost—in those times we recognize, afresh, how dependent we are upon the Lord. We see that we must wait on God to do for us what we cannot do for ourselves.

I can guess that as Ruth waited for Boaz to determine what would happen in her future, she felt the same things we do: uncertainty, fear, anxiety, even hope. Can you picture her pacing the dirt floor of Naomi's home, wringing her hands and praying for God to make his will clear? What *was* God's plan for her life? Would Boaz redeem her? How would it all play out? She had no way to control it, no way of guiding the outcome. She simply had to wait.

> Waiting on God can be a place of great peace.

When I waited to see if my small business would fall apart or sustain our family, I felt the gravity of an outcome that was completely out of my hands. Was this God's plan for our family, or had I missed it? Would we have the provision that we needed, or would everything fall through? How would everything play out? I had to wait.

And yet, in the waiting times of our lives, when every decision and action is out of our hands, there is a gift lingering for us: the opportunity to commune with Christ more deeply. When we are desperate for him to move on our behalf, we see that we are never truly in control, although most of us lean on the illusion that we are.

Waiting on God can be a place of great peace if we turn our attention *away* from whatever we are waiting for—the diagnosis, the job, the relationship, the healing—and turn *toward* the One who holds everything in his hands.

The Lord, who is unchanging, is just as good and faithful in our waiting as he is when our lives seem to be sailing along smoothly. Because "Jesus Christ is the same yesterday and today and forever" (Hebrews 13:8), our souls can be at rest in him, no matter how little we have control over. We do not need to feel overwhelmed: *He* is in control.

Yes, Christ is the one who is in *total* control, and we can trust in him as our truest Kinsman-Redeemer: the one who already paid the highest price for us so that our eternal life could be secure and safe in him. God the Father did not hold back his own Son, but gave him up for us all. "How will he not also with him graciously give us all things?" (Romans 8:32). Focus on the truth of knowing that God is in control—the same God who sees you, knows you, and loves you. Let your heart be at peace in him. He will give you "all things" that you need to follow him today.

- **REFLECT:** When your circumstances feel out of control, you can turn your attention away from the fear and toward the Lord, who has paid the highest price for your heart and life. Ask him to help you focus on Christ today—and to rest in his daily provision for you.

DAY 15

The Peace of God's Abundance

Then the women said to Naomi, "Blessed be the LORD,
who has not left you this day without a redeemer,
and may his name be renowned in Israel!"

Ruth 4:14

• **Read Ruth 4:1-17** •

Ruth looked out the window for the umpteenth time and caught a glimpse of Boaz's outline against the glare of the sun. He was walking toward their home, his head down.

Her stomach flip-flopped and she took a steeling breath. "Lord, help me be strong, whatever news he brings."

Naomi came to stand beside her and hooked their arms together. They watched together as he drew closer, and Naomi's eyes did not waver from the man's face. "He has settled the matter."

"But how, Mother?" Ruth pushed down a shuddering breath and willed her eyes to stop their filling. "My life sits atop a fence, waiting for the wind to blow me one way or the other."

"And the Spirit of the Lord is that wind, daughter."

Ruth's head whipped toward Naomi. "You have not spoken of the Lord's presence for many months." In her anguish and sorrow, her mother-in-law had not mentioned Yahweh except in their Sabbath prayers and duties.

A tear slipped down Naomi's cheek—one she did not move to wipe away. "He is here now, my child. Wait and see."

Within moments, Boaz filled the frame of the home, a tentative smile upon his lips. His eyes rested on Ruth's with affection and joy. "I have redeemed you, my Ruth." He extended a hand to her, his eyes hopeful. "Come and be my wife."

"Boaz!" Ruth rushed past his hand and into his arms. "Yes! With all the joy I can offer!" Boaz lifted her off her toes as Naomi raised her hands with a shout, fresh tears flowing down her face. *God, you have redeemed us! Blessed be the name of the Lord!*

When God provides for us, the peace of his care is as stunning as it is humbling.

On that first day of launching Writing with Grace, I had no idea what was going to happen—and so of course I checked my email approximately every two minutes to see if anyone would purchase a seat in the course. My first purchase came just after 9 a.m., when the website launched. I couldn't believe it! *Someone signed up!*

By noon I had three sign-ups; I was giddy.

By the end of the day, I had twenty. I was amazed.

By the end of launch week? Fifty people had signed up for the first course I ever offered.

I was overwhelmed.

In my heart, I *never* imagined that I would have fifty people sign up for my first online class. It was a university-level course, but they weren't getting any college credits. I was teaching through my own platform, not an online institution or well-known ministry. I had hoped for fifteen, maybe twenty students.

The Lord *blew me away.*

I had spent months worrying and fearing about what would happen with worst-case scenarios. Would Michael have to leave seminary? Would I need to start from scratch and begin a new career path? Would we need to borrow money from family or friends to make it through the end of the year?

And then, in a matter of days, God provided all that we needed for our family to eat and pay rent *for months.* My husband would be able to finish his seminary degree. I could work from home. And best of all? I got to teach others about writing with Christ at the center—my dream and my passion!

For our family, the start of Writing with Grace was a miracle. To this day, I still don't know where all the students came from (some were even from other countries!). And after that initial class, I kept teaching and offering more courses. God's provision through this small business continued throughout Michael's entire time in seminary—it is what kept our family afloat. Through the ups and downs of many years, when we have had no other source of income, the Lord has worked through Writing with Grace to provide for us.

Through Writing with Grace, I have experienced, over and over again, that God is the source of all provision—and peace. I still don't know how most of my students find me or why they decide to take a risk on joining a class with a teacher they've never met! It's a daily reminder to me of God's grace, and that I can trust him to give us what we need, when we need it.

The ultimate blessing of this small business, though, has never been the money (although I'm thankful for it!). The greatest gift has been that I get to partner with others in the work of the kingdom as a fellow disciple and writer: I get to help other writers proclaim Christ's glory through their words!

God's kindness in allowing me to help further the gospel, in some small way, is the greatest treasure I know in my work.

※

When God provided for Ruth, it came in many forms over a long period of time: a mother-in-law who served the one true God, the "coincidence" of gleaning in Boaz's field, the favor of Boaz and the provision of food, and then the amazing gift of Boaz as her kinsman-redeemer. He had been providing for her all along.

It all came to a head the day that Boaz purchased the land that belonged to Naomi's deceased husband and therefore redeemed the land they couldn't afford to keep on their own. With that purchase, he earned the right to marry Ruth and help keep Naomi's family line alive. In one day, Boaz moved Ruth and Naomi out of poverty and into a life of abundance, provision, and hope.

In God's plan, this was not, ultimately, for Ruth to become rich (although God delights in providing for his children). Similarly, her redemption was not only about her happiness (although God delights in the joy of his children). The Lord orchestrated the arc of Ruth's life so that she could partner with him in the story of redemption that God was weaving into the fabric of the world.

> **Any provision we receive is ultimately so that we can leave a lineage of faith.**

The greatest gift she received in her painful, beautiful rescue story is that she got to further the gospel through her life.

Ruth couldn't have known this, of course—her life falls countless years before the birth, death, and resurrection of Christ. But as Boaz's wife, she became the mother of Obed, who became the grandfather of David, who became the king of Israel. It was from that line that Jesus was born.

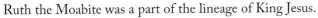

Ruth the Moabite was a part of the lineage of King Jesus.

Her life furthered the gospel even before it was fully known. Her willingness to follow the true God of her mother-in-law, as well as her trust in God's care for her through Boaz, paved the way for her to become a matriarch in the earthly lineage of the Christ. What an immense privilege! What an incredible honor! What abundance!

As you look to God for his provision today, know that he has *true* abundance for you. He is giving you the greatest gift of getting to partner with him in the furthering of the gospel. The practical provision that the Lord gives to us—whether bigger or smaller than we expect—is ultimately so that we can leave a lineage of faith.

Money and homes and cars and things do not last; the gospel will be proclaimed forever.

May our souls be at peace in Christ as we, like Ruth, trust him to lead our lives so that we can be those who leave a heritage of faith and Christ-centeredness in our wake.

• **REFLECT:** Take time today to ask God to help you see abundance the way that he does: not full of earthly treasures, but full of the heavenly treasures of faith, hope, and love. Ask him to help your soul rest in his loving plan for you as you seek to live a life that leaves a heritage of faith.

HANNAH

Peace in Health Trials

DAYS 16–20

DAY 16

Making Peace with Broken Bodies

*He had two wives. The name of the one was Hannah,
and the name of the other, Peninnah. And Peninnah
had children, but Hannah had no children.*

1 Samuel 1:2

• Read 1 Samuel 1:1–5 •

Hannah balled her hands into fists before entering the kitchen, willing herself to keep her spine straight and her eyes dry. She needed to prepare for the journey ahead, and she needed to ignore the sob that was arguing with her throat.

It was time to gather the supplies for their yearly trip to Shiloh.

How many years had she been preparing for this same trip? Peninnah's oldest daughter, Yael, was five years old. . . . That made it eight years of trips. Hannah had married Elkanah nine years ago; two years after that, he had taken Peninnah as his second wife. Peninnah had conceived quickly, and their shared home was soon filled with her two sons and two daughters . . . but none of Hannah's own.

Hannah found herself inadvertently cradling her abdomen and shook her head, trying to shake off the thoughts she could not afford to sit with today.

As she reached for a basket, the sob finally won out. Why was she crying *now*? She drew a deep breath and chided herself. The pain of barrenness was nothing new; she had wrestled with it for years. She should be grateful to get to go on this journey to worship the Lord and sacrifice at the temple. Hannah smoothed her hair back; she *was* grateful. She loved the Lord, and she loved her husband.

But no matter how grateful she was, God still had not answered the one prayer she longed for most dearly—a womb filled with life; a child of her own.

As a new bride, Hannah had assumed she would be pregnant within the first six months of their marriage; when that didn't happen, she believed she would be pregnant within the first year. But as the years bled into each other and Peninnah entered the household, with children coming from her womb in quick succession, Hannah knew it was her body that was broken. The logical thing would be to give up on the hope of having a child.

But she couldn't. No matter how ridiculous it seemed, she couldn't let go of the last shred of hope she clung to. She couldn't stop herself from crying in the night for a child she had never held. She couldn't force her heart to quit praying to the Lord, begging him for just one babe to raise.

The pain of it threatened to undo her as she white-knuckled the basket. She couldn't face Peninnah like this.

Hannah abandoned the hamper and ran to her room.

———

In the years between the birth of our daughter and the birth of our son, I experienced three miscarriages. We hadn't had any fertility issues with Ella, so our struggles were unexpected.

It was my actual pregnancy with Ella that nearly crushed me. I experienced life-altering hyperemesis that required medication and liquid IVs, a mid-pregnancy case of shingles, and sciatica so intense that I was given a state-issued disability tag for my car and often used a wheelchair in my third trimester. The finale of my daughter's birth was an unexpected C-section after a long labor. It seemed fitting.

Still, Ella was happy and healthy. I, on the other hand, was not. I experienced postpartum depression that went undiagnosed for over a year, along with immense fear about going through pregnancy ever again. My body and my mind both felt painfully broken.

But as my daughter started to round the corner toward her third birthday, the desire for another child eclipsed the fear that I had been carrying for so long.

It took us much longer to conceive, though, and when we did, the lives of those precious souls slipped through my body much too soon. Three subsequent pregnancies ended in miscarriage, and I began to wonder if the fears that surfaced during my first pregnancy—that my body was too weak or that I was too broken—might be true.

I was afraid that I had missed my chance for another baby and had messed up my daughter's chance at having a sibling to grow up with in a meaningful way.

I felt that I was failing my daughter, failing my husband, and failing myself.

⸺※⸺

Hannah knew what it was like to feel that her body was failing her. Everywhere she turned in her shared home with Peninnah, children were underfoot—but they weren't her children. Day-to-day life was a reminder of her brokenness, a reminder that the life she wanted was just outside of her reach.

Whether we struggle with physical pain, emotional instability, or mental illness, all of us know what it feels like to live in bodies that feel broken in one way or another. Infertility, depression, anxiety, chronic illness, immunodeficiency, cancer, allergies—these are just a few of the many struggles that we, as humans, face on a daily basis.

And it's hard. So very hard.

Like Hannah, it's hard to live in bodies that don't work and don't seem to measure up. It's difficult to live with brains that don't function the way we want them to. It's challenging to constantly bump up against our limitations and our pains.

Yet there is peace for us in Christ, even in these broken and decaying bodies. Throughout the Word, we see the Lord using men and women whose bodies were imperfect and worn down. Sarah was too old to bear children—she even said her body was "worn out" (see Genesis 18:12)—and yet she birthed a miracle in her old age! Jacob had a permanent limp because he had wrestled with God (see Genesis 32:31), and yet he also *met* with God. Moses struggled to speak, and yet he was the Lord's chosen leader for the Israelites. Elizabeth had been barren for decades until the Lord opened her womb, and she became the mother of John the Baptist (see Luke 1:57–58). Paul had a thorn in his flesh (2 Corinthians 12:7) that the Lord would not take away, but he was still the author of much of the New Testament.

Yes, there is peace for us—a peace that comes from knowing that our hope is not ultimately in the healing of our bodies, but in God himself. For God does not shy away from our broken bodies and weary minds; he loves to show his glory through our weakness!

As we look at the story of Hannah, we see a woman whose infertility brought her great pain and heartache; her soul wrestled with God and others. But what she could not yet know was that even multiple years into her journey with infertility, the Lord was still at work writing a beautiful story for her life. For while her body seemed to be withering, her soul was growing in faith—a faith that we will see poured out beautifully through prayer.

Long before Hannah's exterior life changes, she shows us a glimpse of this biblical truth: "Though outwardly we are wasting away, yet inwardly we are being renewed day by day. For our light and momentary troubles are achieving for us an eternal glory that far outweighs them all" (2 Corinthians 4:16–17 NIV). Even in her "troubles," Hannah was a woman who chose to worship God at his temple. Even as she struggled with infertility and cried over how her life was turning out, she did not turn away from the Lord. She turned *toward* him instead.

If you find yourself wrestling with God today over your broken body, mind, or spirit,

> You can make the choice to turn toward God today in worship and in faith, even if your life is not turning out the way you had hoped.

consider Hannah and the many saints in the Bible who walked with God and found their struggles and weaknesses met by God's grace. Like them, you can experience peace as you make the choice to turn *toward* God today in worship and faith, even if your life is not turning out the way you had hoped.

- **REFLECT:** Today, in your pain, you can choose to turn toward God—and you will find that your heart can be at peace in him, as Paul's was with his own physical pain and weakness: "But [the Lord] said to me, 'My grace is sufficient for you, for my power is made perfect in weakness.' Therefore I will boast all the more gladly of my weaknesses, so that the power of Christ may rest upon me. For the sake of Christ, then, I am content with weaknesses, insults, hardships, persecutions, and calamities. For when I am weak, then I am strong" (2 Corinthians 12:9–10). Take heart and let your soul rest in Christ. The same God of Hannah, Jacob, Moses, Sarah, and Paul is your God too. He is at work in your life—and in your weakness, he is strong.

DAY 17

The Peace That Comes When We Reject Comparison

*So it went on year by year. As often as she went up
to the house of the LORD, [Peninnah] used to provoke her.
Therefore Hannah wept and would not eat.*

1 Samuel 1:7

• Read 1 Samuel 1:4–8 •

Hannah congratulated herself that she had made it through the whole trip to Shiloh without responding to Peninnah's subtle (and not-so-subtle) jabs. That woman was a constant source of distress in her life.

Now it was time to sacrifice to the Lord, and it was the thing that Hannah both loved and hated most of all. She loved that she was able to worship the Lord and make atonement for sin, but she hated how Peninnah taunted her every year. In their shared home, Peninnah was bad enough. But at the temple each year, she let the full measure of her jealous rage fly.

Why? Probably because Elkanah always gave Hannah a double portion to sacrifice, and his love for her was clearly on display. Could she help it that Elkanah loved her more? Hannah knew that she had Elkanah's heart and that Peninnah did not, and that this was the real source of hatred the woman had for her. And that hatred ran deep; Peninnah twisted her anger into a barb that cut to Hannah's most tender place—her barrenness.

As soon as Elkanah left them in the Court of Women, Peninnah's words streamed forth as from behind a door finally unlocked.

She clucked her tongue. "Oh, Hannah. You must need that double portion to atone for so many sins! Everyone knows that children are the sign of God's blessing on women. I wonder what kind of sins you have been hiding, that your womb has always been empty?"

Hannah looked ahead and tried to focus on the sounds of the temple—the words of the priests and hum of people around her. *Yahweh, help me.*

"But the Lord loves me, can't you tell? He has given me so many children that I cannot even fit them in my arms! Two sons for Elkanah and two daughters. Such a *blessing*, don't you think?"

Hannah tried but could not stop the tears from running down her face. Still, she looked ahead and would not respond.

Peninnah dropped her voice to a hiss. "You are a disgrace and a failure as a wife. No man wants a barren woman in his home."

Hannah knew it was true; barrenness was a curse. Peninnah stepped closer to her, whispering lies into her ear. "God has abandoned you, Hannah. Soon Elkanah will too. I give him all that he needs." She spat her last words out with venom. "You offer him *nothing*."

Fear fluttered in Hannah's heart, a caged animal flailing against the bars. Was Peninnah right? Elkanah had no reason to keep her as a wife.

Hannah could not endure it any longer; Peninnah's words cut too deep. She looked down and found her footing, walking away as quickly as she could through tears that blurred her vision. A priest declared God's goodness in the temple, but she could no longer hear the words.

<hr/>

While we were struggling with the grief of our miscarriages, I became acutely aware that we didn't fit the mold of the families around us with children born at an even two-year pace. People constantly asked us if we "only" had one child, and I struggled to answer. While my friends were having their third babies, I was still waiting with an empty womb. One of my closest friends at the time, Laura, was walking with me through our miscarriages and my deep longing for a child; she prayed with and for me regularly. Although we lived in different cities, I was looking forward to making the drive to see her around Christmas.

She already had two children, and they weren't trying for more while her husband was still in seminary. But as soon as I walked into their home that December, she looked at me with tears in her eyes.

"Ann." She didn't even say hello. Her husband sat across the room with a pained look on his face, and I knew what she was going to tell me in a split second. I steeled my heart.

"We're pregnant."

We hugged long and hard, both of us soaking each other's shoulder with tears. She knew what hearing this news would cost me. She knew how dearly I wanted another child—and how they hadn't been planning for this one. "I wanted to tell you in person, because—because I'm sorry. I wish it was you, Ann," she whispered into my ear. "I'm so excited about this child, but I don't want to hurt you."

"I know, Laura." I stepped back long enough to bury my face in my sleeve to try and wipe off the mascara I knew had run down face. "And I'm glad for you, truly. I just—I just want to be able to say the same thing."

Was I happy for them? Of course. But my own sense of loss—and the lack of fairness in it all—overwhelmed my joy for them. I felt so deeply ignored by God, so unseen.

Why, when Michael and I had been crying out for another child, would the Lord bless our friends with a child they weren't even trying to have? Why was it so easy for Laura and so hard for me? What was going on?

⸹

Hannah must have asked the Lord the same questions a thousand times. Why was it simple for Peninnah to have children and so impossible for her? Why did Peninnah have so many children when she couldn't even have one? These questions of comparison often fill our lives: How come she gets to be healthy when I'm fighting a chronic illness? Why does she get to hold down a steady job when anxiety keeps me from functioning? The questions extend beyond our health, of course: Why is she married and I'm not? Why can't I have a better job, like he does? Why is her life so easy when mine is so difficult?

God is at work in your life, and his plans and purposes for you are distinct and important.

Comparison—either from our own hearts or from the mouths of others—is a daily reality for most of us, and it can cause deep pain. We see in Hannah's story that Peninnah's jabs and taunts about her barrenness caused her extreme agony. She wept and wouldn't eat because of her sorrow. The Bible uses strong language to describe the state of Hannah's soul: She was "deeply distressed" and she "wept bitterly." She was "troubled in spirit" with great "anxiety" and "vexation."

This anxiety and vexation can happen to us too, especially when others get what we desperately want. It is then that the voice of comparison can start to weave subtle but troublesome lies into our relationship with God—that perhaps he loves others more than he loves us, or that he listens to others more than he listens to us.

But those lies—which will try to steal your peace—are not the truth. God *is* at work in your life, and his plans and purposes for you are distinct and important. The Bible tells us that "we are his workmanship, created in Christ Jesus for good works, which God prepared beforehand, that we should walk in them" (Ephesians 2:10). He hears you. He sees you. He knows you—and he has not forgotten you.

And so the choice is before us as to whether we will let the lies of comparison keep us in anxiety and fear, or whether we will look to the Lord for our identity and purpose. Paul writes that it is folly to "compare ourselves" with others—something he would not "dare" to do: "When they measure themselves by one another and compare themselves with one another, they are without understanding" (2 Corinthians 10:12).

With God's help, we can choose to walk not in folly, but in truth by belief in his Word, which offers us peace and freedom from comparison.

• **REFLECT:** If you are struggling with comparison that is stealing your peace and joy today, ask God to help you meditate on the truth of his Word—the truth that he is the one who is in control of your life, and that he will see your purposes fulfilled. Meditate on this truth: "The LORD will fulfill his purpose for me; your steadfast love, O LORD, endures forever. Do not forsake the work of your hands" (Psalm 138:8).

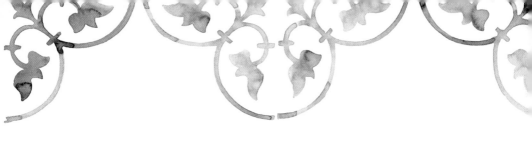

DAY 18

Peace through Prayer

"I have been pouring out my soul before the Lord."
1 Samuel 1:15

• **Read 1 Samuel 1:9–16** •

Hannah managed to sit through half of the family meal before excusing herself. She was so full of grief that her very body felt tied down with weights. Elkanah had coaxed her again and again to eat, but even the smell of the food on the table had made her queasy. It was as if all of the sorrow and anger and angst about her barrenness had poured itself out into her belly and nothing else could fit inside.

She made her way through the city streets toward the temple; her soul was drawn there, to the One who might help her.

No, God had never answered her prayer for a child before, but she could think of nowhere else to turn. Peninnah hated her and would gladly see her suffer. Elkanah loved her but could not open her womb. God was the only one who could free her from the reproach of fruitlessness.

Hannah stopped short of the temple doorposts and knelt outside of the great structure, her body weary with anguish. It was as if a great burden had been laid across her back, one many times too large for her. She could not even lift her head.

She groaned in distress, and prayer cascaded from her lips, although she could not speak the words aloud. She did not have the strength to speak through the tears and sobs that wracked her body. And those tears were bitter in her mouth—she had tasted them too many times to think they might make a difference anymore. Still, if only God would look on her and remember her—and hear her prayer!

She found her voice. "O Lord of hosts, if you will indeed look on the affliction of your servant and remember me and not forget your servant, but will give to your servant a son, then I will give him to the Lord all the days of his life, and no razor shall touch his head." He would be a Nazarite, a man set apart for service to God in the temple. He would belong to the Lord! If only Yahweh would give her a child!

Hannah felt her heart would burst from agony. She wept and wept, her tears turning the dust into mud as she knelt.

Suddenly, she felt a shadow over her, blocking the sun. A voice thick with use spoke in tones that revealed disgust. "How long will you go on being drunk? Put your wine away from you."

Hannah looked up to see the robes of a priest in front of her. Her heart sunk, and she wiped her face before answering. She needed him to see that her eyes were clear. "No, my lord, I am a woman troubled in spirit. I have drunk neither wine nor strong drink, but I have been pouring out my soul before the Lord. Do not regard your servant as a worthless woman, for all along I have been speaking out of my great anxiety and vexation."

The priest looked at her eyes and his eyebrows lifted. Then he nodded, tenderness replacing his anger.

It was after our third miscarriage that I found myself crumpled in a heap in our basement. I had cried more times than I could count in the last year, weeping over the children I'd never had a chance to hold in my arms. But after the loss of this third child, something inside me had shattered beyond the point of recognition; something inside me had died with that babe. I could not string any words together for a long time; I could do nothing but sob. Guttural moans came out, the sounds of a wounded animal that seemed otherworldly even to me. Michael wanted to hold me, but I could not bear any touch. I could not see beyond the clouded veil of tears. I could not even move. I wanted it all to be over—the ache of yearning, the pain of loss, the hope that kept getting dashed every month. No, I did not want to die, but I wanted the overwhelming emotional pain to end.

Logically, I knew that I had mountains of gifts to be grateful for, including a loving husband, a healthy daughter, and a roof over our heads. But I could not see those things then. I could see only one thing—the compounded loss of miscarriage and the dashed hope for another child—and it overtook me.

The work of grieving and pain does not make logical sense. It is the soul's response to loss.

Michael reached out for me as I rolled onto the floor. My husband told me, months later, that he worried I was breaking with reality. I was worried that I was breaking too—fracturing too much to be put back together.

In the silence after my outburst, I had no words—or tears—left. Michael began to pray over me in the fading light that came through the one window in that tiny basement, and I remember feeling a fleeting moment of comfort and peace.

I was at the complete end of myself; all I had left was God.

Hannah shows us that honest prayer is not something that is sterile and sweet. It need not be done in a particular way or offered with the best kinds of words. Instead, her display in front of the temple doors is one of reckless abandon. She is a woman who is utterly desperate for God to help her—and she does not hide her need from him.

Thankfully, the Lord does not despise the prayers that come from an honest heart (see Psalm 51). He *welcomes* them. In fact, it is in the place of honest prayer that God meets us—even in our aching distress—with peace. We see this in the life of Hannah, along with multiple other saints recorded in Scripture who cried out to the Lord in anguish. All of them—including Job, Moses, Elijah, and Habakkuk—were met by God in their pain.

> We never have to to hide our need from God.

But perhaps we see this pattern the most clearly through the psalms of King David. Time and time again, he is distressed and he cries out to the Lord, and God meets him in his agony.

> I am worn out from my groaning.
> All night long I flood my bed with weeping
>   and drench my couch with tears.
> My eyes grow weak with sorrow;
>   they fail because of all my foes.
> Away from me, all you who do evil,
>   for the LORD has heard my weeping.
> The LORD has heard my cry for mercy;
>   the LORD accepts my prayer.
>
> Psalm 6:6–9 NIV

Even through our tears and our sorrow, the Lord hears us. He accepts our prayers.

Yes, my soul, find rest in God;
    my hope comes from him.
Truly he is my rock and my salvation;
    he is my fortress, I will not be shaken.
My salvation and my honor depend on God;
    he is my mighty rock, my refuge.
Trust in him at all times, you people;
    pour out your hearts to him,
    for God is our refuge.

Psalm 62:5–8 NIV

God is our refuge (see also Psalm 46:1), even when our prayers are full of sorrow and distress. Like Hannah, who cried out to the Lord, we can pour out our hearts to God freely. And like King David, we can have a soul that is at peace—a soul that finds its rest in God through prayer, even when those prayers are offered through tears.

- **REFLECT:** In your place of deepest sorrow, God is there, ready to meet you in your distress and weeping. Don't hold back from him today—offer him your true feelings and thoughts, whether good or bad, high or low. The Lord does not despise your honesty; he welcomes it. And as you pour out your heart to him, your soul will find rest—and hope—in God.

DAY 19

Peace in Surrendering to God's Timing

"Go in peace, and may the God of Israel grant you what you have asked of him."

1 Samuel 1:17 NIV

• Read 1 Samuel 1:17–23 •

Hannah looked up at the priest's face and found that kindness had replaced his repulsion.

He raised a hand toward her in blessing, his gravelly voice falling with the weight of thunder on her ears. "Go in peace," he said, "and may the God of Israel grant you what you have asked of him."

Hannah's tears dried even as his words fell. "May your servant find favor in your eyes." A feeling she hadn't known in years filled her: peace. The priest's words had permeated an empty place inside of her; now she knew that God had seen her.

A lightness, like sunshine, filled Hannah's mind. She turned to find Elkanah, knowing that even Peninnah's words could not harm her now. No matter what happened for the rest of her life, she felt in her very marrow that God had not forgotten her.

Two years later

"Are you sure you don't want to make the trip, love?" Elkanah looked at her with tenderness as Hannah nursed their six-month-old son.

Hannah stroked Samuel's cheek as he suckled. How she loved this son that the Lord had given to her. "After the boy is weaned, I will take him and present him before the Lord, and he will live there always." But not yet. "This year, we will stay."

"Do what seems best to you," her husband said. "Stay here until you have weaned him; only may the Lord make good his word."

Elkanah slipped out of the room to continue preparations for the annual trip to Shiloh. Hannah heard the hustle and bustle of Peninnah and her children readying the food and animals, but she didn't move. She was right where she needed to be—here with her son.

—※—

What Hannah did after the priest prayed for her—got up and continued with life—this is what all of us must do at some point or another. We must keep moving forward with our lives, even as physical, emotional, or mental pain nearly overwhelms us. I don't mean that we muscle through and ignore our sorrows—God never asks that of us. And I'm not saying that we don't get the help we need—good doctors and counselors are part of his grace in the world. But, like Hannah, at some point we must get off the ground, surrender our dreams to the Lord, and move on with what must be done.

After my husband prayed for me on the floor of the basement, I had to do this too. Michael had to get back to his seminary class, Ella would be waking from her nap soon, and dinner needed to be made. Yes, it would be frozen pizza, and yes, we would probably spend the evening watching *VeggieTales*, but I had no choice but to keep showing up for my own life.

I turned the oven on and pulled out the paper plates; there would be no energy for washing dishes tonight. After changing into a different shirt—one not smeared with tears and snot—I got my girl up from her bed. We read books on the couch together, and when the oven was hot enough, I slid the pizza in and set the timer. I did all of this with puffy eyes and a heavy heart, but I did it. And in my spirit, I surrendered again to God's plan for my life and for our family, to his ways and his timing. I placed the dreams of having another baby at his feet as I kept doing the things that needed to get done.

This is the hard but true reality of a life lived in surrender to God: We must learn to trust that God is at work in his way and on his schedule, and we must live our lives even as we wait on him.

In the months that followed, this is what I kept doing. I chose to surrender my desire for another child to Jesus. Had I been doing that before? In part. Yes, I had been praying—but I had been clinging to and praying for what *I* thought was best and what I thought *should* be happening in our journey of growing our family. My anxieties and fears—and therefore, my prayers—were based on *my* perspective of the situation, not on God's control over it.

I had to surrender my perspective and choose to trust him.

And as I did so, it was then that I experienced his peace. Because this is what needed to shift in me—I needed to make the *daily* choice to believe that God was sovereign in this painful area of my life, and that he was doing what was best. It was hard to believe that on some days, but I learned that I could make the choice to trust God by submitting my heart to his Word and choosing to follow him—regardless of how he answered my prayer for another child.

This is the place of surrender that all of us must come to when we are waiting on the Lord. After the tears and the groaning, after the yelling and the hurt—we have to decide if we will continue to follow Jesus even if he doesn't answer our prayer the way we want him to.

Hannah made this decision even before her prayer for a child was answered. In the pain and agony of barrenness, she turned toward God rather than away from him. She sought him out and poured her heart out to him. And when she had done all of that, she made the choice to trust him and move ahead: "Then she went her way and ate something, and her face was no longer downcast" (1 Samuel 1:18 NIV).

Peace comes when we surrender our perspective and choose to trust God.

And the Lord gave her a child "in due time" (1 Samuel 1:20)—in the suitable and fitting time, *according to him*. It was not the timing that Hannah had originally prayed for, not on her timeline or within her plans. But it was within God's proper timing, and in his way.

Outside of the temple with Eli the priest, Hannah chose to trust that the Lord heard her and saw her, and that he would do what was best. And then she kept living her life faithfully. When it was due time, God gave her a son.

But we must be careful: This is not a magic formula with the Lord. We cannot think that if we finally get to a place of surrendering our dreams they will automatically be given back to us; faith does not work that way. Many of us will have prayers that are not answered in the way we desire for years, or even for decades.[1] Some of us will pray the same prayers for a

---

1. For more about this topic, see Ann Swindell, *Still Waiting: Hope for When God Doesn't Give You What You Want* (Tyndale, 2017).

lifetime—and we will only see the purposes of those seemingly unanswered prayers in heaven.

God is God. Jesus is sovereign. What he purposes and what he wills are known fully and ultimately only to himself, but we can be at peace knowing that they are good purposes because he loves us: "He who did not spare his own Son but gave him up for us all, how will he not also with him graciously give us all things?" (Romans 8:32).

There is peace in yielding to the Lord and accepting that he is in control of the timing of how prayers are answered in our lives. It is a peace that is hard-won for most of us, grasped through tears and suffering. But it is available to us nonetheless because Christ made it available through his own tears and suffering on the cross. Because Jesus surrendered to the will of the Father and took our sin upon the cross, we can now surrender our desires to the loving Father God who accepts us.

And like Jesus, we can trust that God will do what is best. Even if it feels like death, the Lord is in the business of resurrection.

- **REFLECT:** Where do you need to fully surrender your prayers and your desired timing to Jesus? Is there anything that you have been clinging to that needs to be yielded to him? Ask him to help you make the choice to release your desires to him—and ask him to fill you with his peace as you continue to live your life and do the things that must be done.

DAY 20

Peace through Praise

"My heart rejoices in the LORD;
in the LORD my horn is lifted high.
My mouth boasts over my enemies,
for I delight in your deliverance.
"There is no one holy like the LORD;
there is no one besides you;
there is no Rock like our God."

1 Samuel 2:1-2 NIV

• **Read 1 Samuel 1:24—1 Samuel 2:10** •

Hannah looked around the temple, trusting that she would see the priest who had blessed her nearly four years ago. It was time for her to fulfill her word to the Lord: Samuel would serve in the temple.

She squeezed her son's hand. She would miss Samuel with her entire heart, but she also knew that he belonged here, serving the Lord. It was God who had given him to her, and he was created for God's purposes.

The many nights she had spent praying over her son—and for herself, that she would have the strength to give him back to God—they were being answered now. She felt nothing but peace here with Samuel and Elkanah. This was God's plan for Samuel's life. They had talked with him about it for the last year; he was three years old now and an incredibly bright little boy.

Hannah crouched down to look him in the eyes. "You know that I love you, my son?"

Samuel smiled back at her, his brown eyes full of life. "Yes, Ima. I love you too."

She brushed a curl off his cheek. "And you understand what is happening today?"

"Yes, Ima. I am going to serve the Lord."

She nodded. Now they just needed to find the priest.

There he was! He was a big man, not hard to find. She pointed him out to Elkanah, and the three of them walked toward the man in robes. Hannah could barely keep from yelling.

"Oh, my lord! As you live, I am the woman who was standing here in your presence, praying to the Lord." Her mind flashed back to that day before she gently brought Samuel in front of her. "For this child I prayed, and the Lord has granted me my petition that I made to him. So now I give him to the Lord. For his whole life he will be given over to the Lord."

The priest looked at her with new wrinkles around his eyes. He smiled at Samuel, and then back at her and Elkanah. "I am Eli, and I remember you. So this is your answered prayer, eh? What is your name, little one?"

The boy stood straight and tall, with a confidence that outstripped his age. "I am Samuel."

Eli's eyes widened as he looked at the boy and then placed a trembling hand on Samuel's head. "God's hand is on this child." He removed his hand nearly as quickly as he had placed it there and nodded slowly. "I will care for him as my own son. Come and visit him whenever you desire."

Hannah handed Eli a bag with Samuel's belongings as Elkanah kissed his son and told him he was proud of him. Then Hannah took Samuel in her arms, fresh tears falling down her face. She whispered into his ear, "I love you with my whole heart, and I will always be your Ima. Follow Yahweh, my son. I will visit as often as I can."

Samuel hugged her tightly but was the first to let go. In a way that Hannah couldn't name, she understood, as little Samuel did, that he was created to be here to worship the Lord. The old priest took Samuel's little hand, and the two walked into the temple together. Hannah could no longer see them.

What spilled out of her, then, alongside of her tears, was praise. How kind God had been to her, to take away her reproach and give her a son! He had remembered her!

> "My heart rejoices in the Lord;
> in the Lord my horn is lifted high.
> My mouth boasts over my enemies,
> for I delight in your deliverance.
> There is no one holy like the Lord;
> there is no one besides you;
> there is no Rock like our God...."
>
> 1 Samuel 2:1-2 NIV

My pregnancy with Judah started out as it had with all the other pregnancies we had lost—a faint positive line on a pregnancy test. I remember seeing that pink line pop up and feeling a combination of hope and dread. Hope whispered to my heart that perhaps this child would live long enough in my womb to grow strong and healthy; fear whispered that this precious life would be swept away just as quickly as the others.

Because of the miscarriages I had experienced, any pregnancy I had was automatically considered high risk. I had blood tests right away, took multiple medications, and was watched closely.

My first ultrasound was scheduled as early in the pregnancy as possible, and I was worried. With my daughter's pregnancy, ultrasounds had been rare and exciting; now they were common and nerve-wracking.

The specialist overseeing our pregnancy was a forty-five-minute drive from home, and Michael and I spent most of the trip praying and listening to worship music; it was the only thing that helped to calm my anxious heart. We sang and praised and read Scripture out loud. And as the cornfields marched past our windows, I read Psalm 139 aloud, holding back tears when I came to the middle verses:

> For you formed my inward parts;
>> you knitted me together in my mother's womb.
> I praise you, for I am fearfully and wonderfully made.
> Wonderful are your works;
>> my soul knows it very well.
> My frame was not hidden from you,
> when I was being made in secret,
>> intricately woven in the depths of the earth.
> Your eyes saw my unformed substance;
> in your book were written, every one of them,
>> the days that were formed for me,
>> when as yet there was none of them.
>
> Psalm 139:13–16

I declared the truth about the tiny soul in my womb, not knowing yet if this child was going to live long on this earth. And as I did, my heart was able to praise the Lord and take comfort in knowing that he had ordained every moment and day of this child's existence. Whatever happened at this ultrasound, my soul could rest in knowing that God was in control.

Hannah undoubtedly loved her longed-for son, and yet she also knew, from his conception, that Samuel belonged to Yahweh. In fact, she experienced this reality to a depth that many of us probably cannot imagine. She had promised the Lord that if he gave her a son, that son would serve him at the temple. And by the supernatural grace of God, she fulfilled her word and left Samuel to serve at the temple with Eli.

As she did this heart-wrenching work of relinquishing her son, Hannah miraculously broke into praise! Her prayer is a prophetic one; it is the intertwining of the overflow of her heart and the words of the Holy Spirit.

Hannah's heart "rejoices" in the Lord. She proclaims his holiness and his power to control everything on earth. She knows he alone brings life and death, humility and honor. And without even understanding fully what she is announcing, she points to the coming Messiah—God's "anointed" one (1 Samuel 2:10). But how can Hannah praise the Lord after giving up her son—the very prayer God had answered? She can praise God because she understood that even her very son was ultimately for the Lord, not for herself.

Nothing satisfies our hearts like God.

The same is true for us: Even when we receive what we most desire, whether it is healing or wholeness or a child or a job or a spouse—these gifts are ultimately for the Lord's glory, not for ourselves. This is not because God demands them back from us, like a gift-giver who changes his mind. No—he gives good gifts out of his love for us because he is a good Father (see James 1:17). But everything we have been given must ultimately be entrusted to him, lest we make it an idol that takes the place of the Lord in our hearts.

Nothing satisfies our hearts like God. Hannah knew this. That is why, even as she waved good-bye to her precious son, she could wholeheartedly praise the Lord.

Her praise is even more beautiful when we remember that, in Hannah's world, her son was the outward sign of God's blessing on her life—the erasing of her reproach of barrenness. She could have been afraid that when she "lost" the blessing of Samuel by her side, she would be seen as cursed again. But instead, Hannah declares that she delights in God's deliverance (1 Samuel 2:1). She has already experienced the truth that she is seen and loved by God; she does not need an outward sign to prove it to anyone else.

This is why she can be at peace in her circumstances: She knows that God is with her and for her.

She is satisfied in him.

Nothing on earth will satisfy our hearts like the Lord. Whatever gifts he gives (or doesn't give) us won't fill up our yearning for love or significance or peace. They won't ultimately make us happy. Of course, children and spouses and homes and jobs are blessings from him, and he knows when we yearn for them. But they are not the best gift our souls desire.

What we long for most of all is actually Jesus.

It's only in Christ that our hearts are truly and fully satisfied.

If you feel like you have to give up something you want or love in your life, trust that God is at work. Like Hannah, we can choose to praise the Lord for who he is and for what he has done for us, even after waving good-bye to what we had hoped to keep. The blessings we have on this earth will not last, but the Lord is eternal. He will sustain and keep you, and his presence will be your comfort and your peace.

- **REFLECT:** Take time today to praise the Lord for who he is. Even if you feel that everything has been stripped away, you still have God himself. He is all you truly need, and he can satisfy you today in your longings and fill you with his peace.

Peace in an Unknown Situation

DAYS 21–25

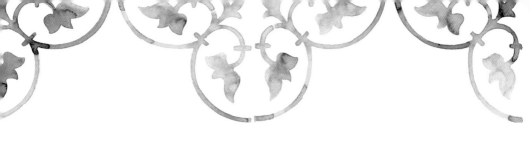

DAY 21

Peace in Accepting God's Will

And Mary said, "Behold, I am the servant of the Lord;
let it be to me according to your word."

Luke 1:38

• **Read Luke 1:26–38** •

Mary took a moment to appreciate the quiet of the morning as she reached for the pestle; it was her turn to grind the grain down to a fine powder. Her mother was visiting a relative across the village with her younger siblings, and Mary was alone to work. Their house was so rarely still.

She sang a psalm quietly as she worked the pestle into the seeds, enjoying the way her words hung in the silence of their small home. Father was in the marketplace as usual—and he would probably see Joseph. Mary's cheeks flushed with warmth. Soon she would be a wife to a good man and have her own home to care for. She was thankful for her betrothal to Joseph. He was not rich, but he was kind.

Suddenly, the home filled with a brightness that temporarily blackened her vision, and Mary's skin tingled with the warmth of a gentle fire. As her eyes adjusted, she saw a being unlike anything she'd ever known filling the room with his presence, and she flung herself to her knees.

"Greetings, you who are highly favored!" His voice resonated like a struck bell, filling her very bones with his clear, pure tenor. "The Lord is with you."

She hesitated before looking up, and when she did, tears filled Mary's eyes. This was no man. She shuddered; this was a messenger of God, and to see the glory of God was to die!

It was as if the being knew her very thoughts. "Do not be afraid, Mary; you have found favor with God." His eyes were kind even in their ferocious beauty. "You will conceive and give birth to a son, and you are to call him Jesus. He will be great and will be called the Son of the Most High. The Lord God will give him the throne of his father, David, and he will reign over Jacob's descendants forever; his kingdom will never end."

Mary's heart thrilled at the words even as she struggled to make sense of them. A son? She had never known a man.

She found her voice. "How will this be, since I am a virgin?"

The angel smiled at her, his joy scattering like raindrops from a shaken leaf. "The Holy Spirit will come upon you, and the power of the Most High will overshadow you. So the holy one to be born will be called the Son of God. Even Elizabeth, your relative, is going to have a child in her old age, and she who was said to be unable to conceive is in her sixth month!"

Mary gasped. Elizabeth? Pregnant at her age? The angel nodded at her. "For nothing will be impossible with God."

Twin emotions grappled in Mary's heart—fear and wonder. *How can this be? How can I be the mother of God's Son? And—oh! What will Joseph think?* But her momentary fear was overtaken by the thrill of God's presence in the room. There was peace here, and a deep well of joy she had never experienced before.

"I am the Lord's servant," Mary answered, bowing her head to the ground. Her knees had never left the dirt. "May your word to me be fulfilled."

When she looked up, the angel was gone.

When we are faced with an unknown situation, it can be challenging to trust the Lord—especially when we don't know what's up ahead. It can be hard to walk in peace when the circumstances we find ourselves in are uncertain and unclear, or overwhelming and obtuse.

I found myself struggling to walk in peace in the months after Michael was fired, in part because one fear dominated most of the others I was facing: the fear of moving again. We had already moved three times in three and a half years, and I was determined to stay put. I didn't want to uproot our kids again, I didn't want to uproot myself again, and I was scared of starting over yet another time. Emotionally, all of the moves had worn me out. Practically, the thought of packing up boxes again made me feel nauseous.

So we kept Michael's job search local. But after a couple of months of fruitless searching, I begrudgingly said that I *might* be okay if we extended our search and at least stayed in the state, as long as we were within driving distance of family.

Still, I was holding out for something nearby. In my heart, I had put my foot down; I was *not* going to move.

And then we had friends who mentioned an opening at their church in Michigan. I laughed. Michael told them that the likelihood of our moving across the country again was almost nonexistent, but that—*sure*—they could share his résumé with the pastor if they wanted to.

That résumé led to a phone call, which led to another phone call, which led to a staff Zoom interview, which led to an elder interview. This church in Michigan was interested in hiring my husband.

I found myself at an emotional crossroads.

In my heart, I had already said no to anything other than staying in Texas. I prayed and prayed that God would keep us where we were so that our kids wouldn't have to start over yet again.

But every other option fell away like the petals of a dying rose.

I found myself praying a new prayer: that God would help me to say yes to what he was requiring of us. My desire to stay put was eclipsed by my longing to follow the Lord, and so if he was calling us to Michigan, I wanted to be able to go with a willing heart.

Scholars imagine that Mary was only a teenager when the angel Gabriel visited her with his heavenly news that upended her life. I try to imagine the moment when the angel appeared to a young girl who was offered the most unbelievable of invitations. It was, humanly speaking, impossible: The God of the universe invited her to carry the hope of the world in her womb.

Mary's response shocks and stills me.

Her response, unwavering and clear-voiced, rings off the pages of Scripture: "Behold, I am the servant of the Lord; let it be to me according to your word" (Luke 1:38).

Her answer is completely about *God*. It is not about what she wants or hopes for; it is about who God is and what he has planned.

And this is not a flippant response. Mary would have understood that God was not only asking her to carry Jesus; he was asking her to lose her worldly status and, most likely, her fiancé. For who would believe that she had remained true to Joseph as her womb swelled with life?

In the moment that the angel Gabriel arrives, Mary learns that God is giving her a strange blessing—one that will make her stand out and be questioned, bring pain and probably persecution.

But this teenager, she humbles me. With all the ramifications of the invitation in front of her, she accepts God's extended hand.

Mary says yes.

And in her yes, she partners with God to usher the Prince of Peace—our Savior—to earth.

Like Mary, each of us is daily invited to accept God's invitation to partner with him in ushering the kingdom of heaven to earth.

But that invitation often comes through unknown situations where we have to trust him and give him our yes *before we can see the outcome.*

For me, that meant yielding my desires to God's call. Although I wanted to stay in Texas, it became crystal clear that we were meant to move to Michigan.

And so I read the Bible. I read about Mary and her confident yes to God, even though she must have lacked much confidence about what that obedience meant for her day-to-day life.

Her faithfulness helped me to make the choice to obey God through my actions (I got out the packing boxes again) and my words (I spoke words of hope and joy about Michigan even in the unknown).

When we say yes to God, we will find that he provides all that we need in him.

And the Lord met my small actions of obedience with his peace.

I still didn't know how everything would work out. Would my daughter struggle with a new life in a new town? Would the job work out? Would we make new friends? There were no guarantees—but my soul was able to rest in God's sovereignty and in his plan for us as I chose to obey him.

Sometimes in big ways—but often in small ones—God invites us to say yes to him in unknown circumstances. Maybe it's through something big, like taking a new job. Or maybe it's through something small, like reaching out to make a new friend. Maybe it's sharing the gospel with a neighbor, or maybe it's giving away more money than you usually would. Maybe it's fostering a child, or maybe it's choosing to love the children you have with contentment and joy. There are a million ways that God asks us to trust and obey him—and a million opportunities for us to say yes to him again.

Like Mary, we will find that as we say yes to the Lord, we experience his peace. But that will not often be because of the circumstances; it will be because his presence is *with* us in the circumstances.

As we accept the invitation that God extends to us today to obey him wholeheartedly, even in unknown situations, we will find that he provides all that we need in him (Matthew 6:33), along with the peace to move forward in his strength.

All we need to say is yes.

• **REFLECT:** How is the Lord inviting you to say yes to his will today? In what area do you need to trust him to provide peace as you walk forward into a new situation? Write those things down and ask God to help you say a wholehearted yes to him today!

DAY 22

Peace through God's Help

When Joseph woke from sleep, he did as the angel
of the Lord commanded him.

Matthew 1:24

• **Read Matthew 1:18–25** •

Mary braced herself. Joseph would walk through their door any moment, either to divorce her or marry her. What would he choose? Her stomach whipped with anxiety. *O Lord, help me. I do not want to raise your Son alone.*

Mary replayed the events of the last week in her mind.

She had been so hopeful to see Joseph when she returned from her visit with Elizabeth—her cousin who had given birth to a baby boy in her old age! But Mary was visibly pregnant now, the swell of her womb unavoidable under her dress. And when Joseph saw her, his face fell like granite from the side of a mountain.

He had clenched his jaw in the same way her own father had when she'd returned home the day before, and, like her father, Joseph had asked for an immediate explanation. She told her fiancé the same thing she had told her own parents, relaying the angelic message with clarity and conviction.

Joseph's face had gone from stony to blank. Mary longed to read his mind.

He had said one thing—and he said it to her father rather than to her: "I will pray, and I will return in one week to disclose what I will do."

There were only two choices, she well knew: divorce or marriage. Divorce would ruin her reputation even more, if that were possible. But marriage would ruin his, for everyone would assume his marriage was an acknowl-edgment that he was the babe's father.

The same prayer rose in her heart that she had repeated a thousand times over the last week. *Lord, help. Help Joseph to know the truth.*

Joseph's shadow lengthened in the doorframe before he entered. She stole a glance at her betrothed, but his eyes were unreadable.

Mary's father nodded at Joseph with pain in his eyes. She knew her father loved her, but she could tell he did not believe her. Who would? Had she not been the one who was pregnant, she might never have believed the angel's words either.

Joseph looked at her father before shifting his gaze to her. There was a softness there, plus something she hadn't seen before: determination.

"I will marry your daughter, sir." His eyes remained locked on Mary.

Her father released a breath she hadn't realized he was holding.

"You are sure about this, Joseph?"

He turned to his new father-in-law. "Completely, Father. Your daughter speaks the truth." He looked at her again, a weighty smile on his face. An angel of the Lord came to me in a dream last night. She carries the Savior of our people, put there by the Holy Spirit."

Mary held back a sob but couldn't stop the tears from pooling in her eyes. *O Lord! You have told him! Thank you!* Joseph extended his arm to her. "Come, Mary. Be my wife."

She shed the fear she had been carrying since the day the angel visited her and stepped toward her husband. God had heard her prayer.

Have you ever found yourself in a circumstance where you don't even know what to pray for? Perhaps there is a relationship that needs mending, but it's tricky to know where to start. Maybe there's financial strain, but it's difficult to imagine how it could be fixed. Or possibly there is physical healing that's needed, but the diagnosis makes you wonder if prayer will even help. Whatever it is, the situation feels overwhelming, and you don't know how to petition God for help.

I can imagine that after Mary's encounter with the angel Gabriel, she found herself constantly asking God for help. But I also wonder if she struggled to verbalize what *kind* of help she needed; her circumstance was utterly unique in the history of the world. Perhaps many of her prayers were simple: *Lord, help me.*

Sometimes, this is the only prayer we have to offer. The Lord understands this—he has even made provision for us in our confusion and weakness: "Likewise the Spirit helps us in our weakness. For we do not know what to pray for as we ought, but the Spirit himself intercedes for us with groanings too deep for words" (Romans 8:26).

God, help us. I've arrowed this prayer to heaven too many times to count. When our son was so sick: *God, help us.* In our deep grief after loss: *God, help us.* After Michael was fired and we were struggling in every area, sometimes *God, help us* felt like the only prayer I could offer. When my words were spent, when I couldn't muster the energy or the hope to pray, *Help* was what came out of my heart.

God responds to this prayer, just as he responds to every prayer of all his children. We can't always see it in the moment, but the Lord is constantly working on our behalf. He is *always* interceding for us (see Hebrews 7:25; Romans 8:34).

And often, God's help comes through the hands of others—through meals and conversations, through shared tears and the gift of understanding. He uses his own body—the body of Christ—to help where it's needed most. We had doctors who helped us with Judah's medical issues. We had friends who prayed with us and brought us meals after our miscarriages. And we experienced the beautiful help of Christ through a ministry that I'd never heard of: the Pastors' Hope Network[1]—a national ministry specifically for pastors who have been fired or forced to resign. From emotional support to covering counseling costs, from résumé services to financial guidance, Deanna and her team helped us immensely after Michael's job loss.

In those circumstances (and too many more to mention), we often prayed the simple prayer of *God, help us*—and through the love and kindness of his people, we experienced peace in every difficult season.

Mary did not have handrails for what she was walking through as a young and unwed mother to the Savior of the world. But as she trusted God for his help—and surely prayed for his help too many times to count—she saw him care for her through others.

Be at peace: God is always helping us.

This is what God does over and over again: he uses his people to help care for his people. He allows his children to point to the pathway that helps hurting people find peace.

This is what Joseph did for Mary, in so many ways. God spoke to Joseph about the truth of Jesus' conception through a dream, and he believed. In

1. Pastorshope.net

taking Mary home to be his wife, he shouldered the burden that she would have otherwise carried alone. The shame that her culture would have put on her as an unmarried pregnant woman? He took that away when he took her as his wife. The fear of raising a child by herself? He took that burden from her when he married her. The anxiety of navigating her new life? Joseph brought peace with him when he agreed to take her as his bride.

Joseph was, indeed, a "righteous man" (Matthew 1:19 NLT)—one who trusted and obeyed God rather than looking to what others might think of him when he did so.

And Joseph's righteousness in obeying the Lord paved the way for peace between not only himself and Mary, but for peace in the whole world. Because he believed God (and therefore believed Mary), they had peace in their marriage. And because he was willing to shoulder the burden and gift of raising Jesus, the two of them helped bring the Prince of Peace into the world.

In seasons of difficult circumstances, don't hesitate to pray the simple prayer of *Lord, help*. And then? Keep your eyes open for God's comfort and help in your life—being "watchful and thankful" (Colossians 4:2 NIV). It may not come through the people you expect or in the way you thought it would, but he is *always* helping us. Mary had to give her fears about an unknown future to God, and she found herself helped by God through Joseph. Joseph had to cast his concerns about Mary and their life together to God—and God helped him through a dream that gave him the confidence he needed to move forward. Like Mary and Joseph, we who are his children will also receive his help in our time of need. "God is our refuge and strength, a very present help in trouble" (Psalm 46:1).

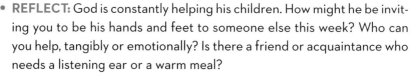

- **REFLECT:** God is constantly helping his children. How might he be inviting you to be his hands and feet to someone else this week? Who can you help, tangibly or emotionally? Is there a friend or acquaintance who needs a listening ear or a warm meal?

  If you feel like you are not experiencing God's help in the situations where you need peace today, meditate on Psalm 46:1–3 and Romans 8:28. He is working in your life. Ask the Lord for eyes to see his help for you afresh.

DAY 23

Peace in God's Unlikely Orchestration

And she gave birth to her firstborn son and wrapped him
in swaddling cloths and laid him in a manger,
because there was no place for them in the inn.

Luke 2:7

• Read Luke 2:1–7 •

Mary white-knuckled her dress and tried to breathe. Joseph was running like a madman through the streets of Bethlehem, and she could no longer follow. She was leaning against the wall of one of the many inns that were overfull; the census had filled this town with travelers like bees in a hive.

She stifled a groan and waited for the contraction to finish its mighty pulse. She thought she had at least two weeks until the babe would make his appearance, but it was very clear that he was coming now. Here? Away from their home and her family? She could have cried, but every ounce of energy within her was already focused like a beam of light on the power rolling through her body.

Where is Joseph? He'd been gone probably ten minutes, but it felt like hours. He had relatives in this town, but their homes were already full. There was no room for the two of them—soon to be three of them—to stay.

He rounded the corner, the whites of his eyes reflecting off the setting sun. "Mary? Are you all right? I found a place for us, but I'm sorry—"

She grabbed his hands and tried to stand up fully. "Just—take—me."

Joseph half guided, half carried her down the long street to a home she didn't know. Mary clenched her teeth as another contraction nearly brought her to her knees; Joseph waited and held her until it passed.

She looked up the stairs that led into the family quarters. "They made room"— she found her breath—"for us?"

Joseph dipped his head, trying to keep her from seeing the tears in his eyes. "Downstairs, my love."

Where they kept the animals?

"I'm sorry, Mary. It is all the space that is left."

She shook her chin. *God, what is going on? Surely you don't want your Son born among the donkeys?*

A throaty cry tore from her as another wracking contraction rippled through her middle. Joseph picked her up and carried her into the darkness below. It was time for Jesus to come into the world.

⚯

It was the November when our daughter was six months old that my husband started experiencing unexplainable nausea and blinding headaches. We had no idea what was happening, and we were confused—and scared. His pain was so severe that we landed in the emergency room multiple times; one doctor thought he might have viral meningitis, another thought adult-onset migraines, and yet another claimed it was some unknown condition. No one had answers.

Around the same time, I suddenly started experiencing vertigo so intense that I felt unsafe holding the baby and sometimes couldn't stand upright for more than a few seconds. When I saw a physician, he told me there was no way to know where vertigo originated from, and to wait it out.

I stood in the parking lot after that doctor's appointment and wept. *God, what is going on? Can no one help us? We need you to help!*

We were new parents, and I was starting to think that we might be crazy. Maybe the lack of sleep was leading us to create symptoms that weren't real? Maybe we were losing our minds?

But not long after that desperate prayer, we received two phone calls within twenty-four hours—one call from Michael's mom, and one call from mine. Individually, and without talking to each other, each of them asked if we had checked the carbon monoxide levels in our home.

I told my mom that we had two carbon monoxide detectors in our house, and that neither had gone off. But after my mother-in-law called to ask the same question, I looked online at the side effects of carbon monoxide poisoning. Goosebumps slid up and down my arms: dizziness, relentless headaches, vomiting.

We called an HVAC technician, who came and discovered that our furnace had broken down in key places, pumping carbon monoxide levels into our condo higher than what is legally allowed in parking garages. We were sick because we were experiencing low-grade carbon monoxide poisoning.

Michael had the worst of it, and he ended up needing oxygen therapy for a while. But it could have been so much worse. God had orchestrated events in order to spare our lives before the carbon monoxide levels became deadly. He used the responses of our bodies, heard the prayers of our hearts, and gave supernatural insight to both of our mothers—all in his sovereign plan to help and heal us. Although it didn't feel like help at the time, the sickness that we experienced was the only way we could have discovered the deadly poison leaking through our home.

When Mary gave birth to Jesus in the same place where animals slept and ate, I have to guess that she was troubled. No woman longs to give birth around barn animals (perhaps especially the woman who is birthing the king of the world)! I wonder if she merely questioned the situation they found themselves in or worried that they had somehow missed God's plan for Jesus' birth. Because surely—*surely* God's best for them would not include Jesus being born away from their home, her family, and all they knew? Surely God did not want her to welcome the Savior into the same hay where animals rolled?

> **The Lord is orchestrating events in your life for your good and for his glory.**

Yet God knew what Mary and Joseph could not have seen fully at the time: that Jesus' birth in a town not their own—but in Bethlehem—fulfilled the words of the prophets. God knew that Christ's birth without fanfare in a peasant community proclaimed his humble presence with his people, and that Immanuel had come to dwell in human form. God knew that proclaiming the coming of the Savior to nearby shepherds (and not to royal kings or those of import) was a sign that the Savior was for *all* who would receive him.

Mary's difficult circumstance in Bethlehem, away from all that she knew (and probably different from all that she had hoped for with Jesus' birth), had been orchestrated by God for her good and for Christ's glory. The census that called them away from home got them to where they needed to be. The full houses and inns led them to a humble dwelling where the king of the universe did not shy away from the neediness and mess of his people. Every detail that Mary did not understand—all of it was for the sake of the gospel going forth in the world.

The Scripture tells us that after Jesus' birth and the coming of the shepherds to worship, "Mary treasured up all these things, pondering them in her heart" (Luke 2:19). What had first probably seemed confusing to her became a "treasure" to her heart. She rested in the fact that God was with her, and that this was all in his plan.

When you find yourself in a set of circumstances that don't seem to make sense or that bring you anxiety and fear, know that God is sovereign. He is orchestrating events in your life for your good and for his glory. Ask God to help you treasure up his work and ponder it in your heart, and then let your soul rest. The king of the world is with you, and his plan is working itself out in perfect timing in your life.

• **REFLECT:** Your life is under God's careful orchestration. Let your soul be at peace; the same God who cared for Mary and Joseph is at work in your life too. Ask him to help you treasure up his good work in your heart as you learn to trust him more.

DAY 24

Peace When the Worst Comes

When Jesus saw his mother there, and the disciple whom
he loved standing nearby, he said to her, "Woman, here is
your son," and to the disciple, "Here is your mother."
From that time on, this disciple took her into his home.

John 19:26–27 NIV

• Read John 19:25–30 •

Mary closed her eyes to remember him as he had been, whole and healthy, preaching on hills and in deserts, along lakeshores as well as in temple courts. In her heart, Mary believed that Jesus was the King of the kingdom of God come to earth. She had experienced it through his conception, and had seen the truth even in his days as a babe when he toddled around their home with grace and insight beyond his age. She had seen it in his kindness extended to others since his youth, in his wisdom and passion for the Torah. And in the last three years, she had seen the kingdom blossom from within him, a living well of water for all who heard and responded to his words. Jesus carried God's presence. He was the Messiah.

So what was happening now? Her son, the Christ, tortured and hung on a cross? *God! Hear us and have mercy on us!*

Mary's sorrow ran so deep that she feared she might die with him. Pushing down the bile in her throat, she readjusted her feet. She had already retched twice this day but was determined to be near her son when he died. *O God! How can this be your will?*

Tears ran rivulets down her cheeks, but the horror of what was in front of her had silenced her sobs. Jesus—her Jesus, her precious son—was dying in fathomless pain. Blood ran from his back, his head, his hands, and his worn feet. How there was any left to come out bewildered her; he had lost so much that his face was pale as linen.

She reached out to him as he hung there on the cross, aching to hold her son. But he was impossible to embrace, and she saw—or perhaps she felt—that the pain he carried could not be shared.

Lord! Have mercy on your child! You said he would rule and reign, that he would have a kingdom. But he is bleeding to death!

Even as her soul cried out in prayer, her mind tried to grasp reality. Her son really was dying, as far from a throne as could be imaginable. She watched Jesus' shuddering chest rise and fall as he fought for breath, and his words from these last years flitted through her mind in snatches.

Repent, for the kingdom of heaven is at hand.

The kingdom of heaven has suffered violence.

Blessed are the poor in spirit, for theirs is the kingdom of heaven.

She searched his beloved face, now mottled with pain and determination. A thought came to her, unbidden: *He knows what he is doing.*

It was then that Jesus' eyes fluttered open, and he nodded to her and then looked to John, who was standing next to her. His voice, withered and dry, came over her as a blessing.

"Woman, here is your son." The pain and effort of speech shuddered through him. Then, to John: "Here is your mother." He nodded back to

Mary. John reached for Mary's hand and held it, though neither took their eyes off of Jesus. "Yes, Rabbi. I will care for her as my own mother." She squeezed John's hand and whispered, "Thank you, my son."

Even now Jesus was caring for her. *Oh! How she loved him!*

It is common to fear the worst happening in our lives; most of us could name our greatest fear without thinking too hard. Perhaps it is losing your spouse or child. Perhaps it is losing your home or your job. Perhaps it is great physical pain or sickness.

I have friends who have lost children to cancer and spouses to early death. I know many whose marriages have been destroyed by infidelity or distrust. Dear friends lost their home and everything in it to fire. I have seen my own parents walk through betrayal and the loss of community. Michael and I have experienced miscarriages, job loss, and depression. And this is just in our small circle of life. You can surely name your own hurts and losses, as well as those of the people you know.

Life includes great pain and hardship for all of us; no human escapes the grasp of sin, fallenness, and death.

But even when the worst happens to us or those we love—*even then*, God knows what he is doing. This does not mean that God created the evil or the pain or the darkness that we walk through. He is solely good:

> "The Rock, his work is perfect,
>   for all his ways are justice.
> A God of faithfulness and without iniquity,
>   just and upright is he."
>
> Deuteronomy 32:4

Let no one say when he is tempted, "I am being tempted by God," for God cannot be tempted with evil, and he himself tempts no one. (James 1:13)

God is just, upright, faithful, and perfect. He never tempts us or creates evil. No matter what happens, he is still in control, and he sees and knows how he will redeem your greatest pain.

The same God who redeemed even the cross can—and will—redeem all the sorrows and suffering you have experienced.

Mary experienced this firsthand, as no other person on earth had. As the mother of Jesus, and also as one of his faithful disciples, she loved him perhaps more intimately than any other human. For who knows a child like his own mother? She had kissed his scrapes and cradled him in her arms. She had seen him grow and had humbled herself to learn from him. She was a woman of great faith and faithfulness, and yet the worst imaginable thing happened in her life—her son was murdered for sins he never committed.

Her pain crushed her.

God did not save Jesus from the cross. She watched her son die on that old, rugged cross without any seeming intervention from heaven. All the dreams and hopes and promises she had from God—the ones spoken by the angel before he was born—seemed to disintegrate in front of her as he died.

What she saw seemed hopeless.

But even in his death, Jesus honored his mother by caring for her. He knew that she would need a physical home as she aged, along with an earthly family to love her and provide for her. And so he commanded John to take Mary in as his mother, which John did. Even in and through Mary's worst, Jesus was caring for her and providing for her. He made sure she was never alone.

When you go through your worst—whatever that is—remember Mary. Remember that although what she saw seemed hopeless, *Jesus knew what he was doing*. She did not, but he did.

There was a plan at work that she could not yet understand; God was going to redeem that *worst* and make it the greatest victory in the history of the world through Christ's resurrection only three days later. The *worst* would become the *best*—the defeat of sin and death for all time.

Your worst may not turn around in three days; it may never fully change here on earth. But again, remember Mary. Jesus took care of her by providing a home and family for her even as he was dying; she was never far from his heart. He is doing the same for you. You are never far from his heart—in fact, you are held close and loved by him at every moment. Even in the worst days of your life, God sees you and is caring for you, providing you with the peace and comfort that you need to make it through to the next moment.

> The worst that can happen here on earth will be redeemed in and through Christ.

And because of what Christ has already accomplished through his death on the cross and his victorious resurrection, the worst days that you experience here on earth will ultimately be redeemed—either on earth or in heaven. Every pain and hurt and horror you have walked through will be healed and made whole and restored when Christ comes to make all things new (see Revelation 21:5). Every single one.

Let this reality offer your heart peace. The worst that can happen here on earth will be redeemed in and through Christ. You are loved and held close by God. As he did for Mary, he will care for you and provide for you even as you walk through pain. You are never alone.

- **REFLECT:** When you fear (or even experience) the worst, ask God for the peace that comes from the truth that he knows what he is doing. Peace comes as we recall that he has already taken on the worst of sin and suffering through the cross. Read John 19 to meditate on what he endured out of love for you, and ask him to help you trust him as you walk through your own trials, remembering that he will never leave you or forsake you (see Deuteronomy 31:6; Hebrews 13:5).

DAY 25

Peace in a New Reality

All these with one accord were devoting themselves to prayer,
together with the women and Mary the mother
of Jesus, and his brothers.

Acts 1:14

• **Read Acts 1:1–14** •

Mary looked around the room in wonder. Not even two months ago, they had all been together to weep and mourn the death of her son. They thought all had been lost—that every promise Jesus made had gone unfulfilled.

How wrong they had been! The room broke out in a song that Thomas had recently crafted about faith in their Lord, and her mind wandered back. Her heart thrilled at the memories of those days. Jesus had risen, as he said! She had hugged him and cried with joy over him. And now that he had returned to heaven, they were worshiping him—their risen Lord Jesus, who had defeated death after three days in his borrowed tomb.

Grateful tears pooled in her eyes as she closed them again, joining the other disciples in song and thanksgiving. *God, your works are too wonderful for me. Thank you for letting me be here. Thank you for giving me a front-row seat to Jesus all his life. Thank you for the Messiah!*

He had truly come and saved them, the Messiah she had carried! She had never doubted that Jesus was God's son, but these last weeks had crystallized his purpose in her heart. He had not come to set up an earthly kingdom, as she had once assumed. No, his plan was different. The disciples had all been talking about it together, going over the prophecies that Jesus had fulfilled and the words he had spoken to them. Jesus had come to set up a heavenly kingdom and bring his salvation to earth. By dying for the sins of all, he remade the pathway to Yahweh.

Mary's breath caught. These moments happened often in the upper room where they met; the presence of God felt tangible. It reminded her of Gabriel's announcement so many years ago. She felt herself reaching out, as if she could grasp God's nearness with her hands.

What she felt instead was a burning in her very heart. Jesus *was* the Messiah—the Christ! He was truly victorious and would return from his heavenly throne. Her mother's heart was tender. *I hope you will return soon, Lord. But I trust you no matter what.*

She did trust him now, more fully than ever before. He had been her son, but he was also her Lord. And now, she was his grateful disciple. What did that mean for her? She wasn't sure. What would change? She had no idea. But she knew that no matter what, she would follow Jesus as a disciple forever, even as she prayed for his return.

Think about the times in your life when you suddenly faced a new reality. Perhaps your world shifted after an unexpected diagnosis, after the loss of a loved one, or after the decision a spouse, child, or employer made. Or perhaps you got a new job or moved to a new city. Perhaps the shift was more subtle—but no less important—after the death of a dream or the loss of some part of your external identity.

Mary faced a new reality when Jesus defeated sin and was raised from the dead. Now he was not only a well-known rabbi who was her son; his resurrection demonstrated that he was clearly the Messiah and king of heaven. While the Scriptures infer that she always believed in him and followed his teaching (Luke 8:19–21), his resurrection shaped a new reality not only for Mary, but for the entire world. Things had changed drastically.

Mary found herself in a new reality in which her primary role shifted to living as a disciple of Christ. She could not have yet known what that would mean for her; Jesus' resurrection and victory over death was brand-new for everyone! While she could have responded to this change with anxiety and fear, refusing to move into a new season of her life, the Scriptures show us that she moved forward and wholeheartedly gave herself to this new calling.

In fact, Mary was in the thick of the disciples who comprised those early followers after Jesus ascended into heaven (see Acts 1:14). She was most likely there when the Holy Spirit fell on the believers at Pentecost and they spoke in tongues (see Acts 2:1–4), and she surely continued to follow Christ for the rest of her days.

Her reality shifted dramatically, but Mary continued to put Jesus at the center of her life.

Mary's example is one for us to follow. We all face new realities at different junctures in our lives, and what may feel immensely stressful for one person may seem relatively inconsequential for others.

Becoming a mom was a radical change for me, and my reality shifted enormously. After seven years of marriage without kids, the change to becoming a parent, while not unexpected, was a drastic shift. I'd seen other friends become mothers without blinking—they seemed to melt into their new role perfectly, without fears or struggles. I, on the other hand, was a mess. I adored my child but wrestled with feeling trapped by motherhood and overwhelmed by the demands it necessitated. Peace was hard to come by in my early months of motherhood.

But I still had the choice: Would I put Christ at the center of my life, or not? Would I choose him in the midst of my new reality, or would I let other things dominate my days?

I tried to choose Christ as much as I could. I remember the newborn days when I didn't actually crack open my Bible until 5 or 6 p.m., even though I'd been trying since I woke up. I determined that I would do it, no matter how long it took me every day. And in those moments when I read the Word, I found my heart flooded with peace. The rest of those early days were filled with tears from the baby (and me) as I tried to navigate sleep, nursing, and recovering from the birth. But when I opened the Word and refreshed my heart in the truths of Scripture, I found myself anchored in a truth that never changed, regardless of what was changing in my life.

This is what Mary chose: to anchor herself in Truth himself. As the world she knew changed profoundly because of the resurrection—and the persecution of the early church—she steeped herself in worshiping the Lord and prayer. And with the New Testament yet unwritten, Mary and the other disciples surely reminded themselves of the words of Christ and encouraged each other with his words, along with the Old Testament prophecies that pointed to him. In the midst of monumental change, their hearts found peace in God.

> When our life changes, we can choose to anchor ourselves in the truth of Christ.

Today, in whatever change you are facing, you can choose to anchor yourself in the truth of Christ. Recount his words. Sing about him. Pray by yourself and with other believers. Yes, our reality in this world will constantly morph and shift for as long as we have breath. But Christ is unchanging. He is the Truth, and as we cling to him, we will find the peace that we need to face whatever is ahead—just as Mary did.

- **REFLECT:** In a constantly changing world, Christ is stable and secure (see Hebrews 6:19). He is constant and faithful. Just as Mary chose to continue to follow Jesus into the new reality of life without him physically on earth, we can choose to continue to follow him as we face new experiences—because as believers, we carry his Holy Spirit with us forever! Immerse yourself in his Word today and let your soul rest in his constancy and goodness, no matter what you face.

THE
DISCIPLES

Peace in Difficult Relationships

DAYS 26–30

DAY 26

Friends, Enemies, and Peace

*When morning came, he called his disciples to him and chose
twelve of them, whom he also designated apostles.*

Luke 6:13 NIV

• Read Luke 6:12–16 •

Andrew cringed. This was *not* going to work.

Next to him, his brother Simon was silently seething; the throbbing visible in his neck was the telltale sign Andrew had learned from their shared childhood.

Andrew looked around the small circle. His fellow fishermen, James and John, were talking to each other, trying to ignore the tension in the air. At least he knew them, even if they *were* competition on the water. Several of the men were strangers to him. He thought he'd seen the tall guy before but didn't know his name.

Everyone knew Matthew, of course, whether they wanted to or not. He was a tax collector. Andrew noticed that although Matthew held his head high, a trickle of sweat rolled past his ear. He was nervous. Andrew didn't blame him for that: nobody liked Matthew, least of all Simon the Zealot. *A Zealot!* Bringing those two men within a street of each other was insanity. Andrew had no idea what Jesus was thinking.

Unintentionally, Andrew took a small step back. His brother was a dangerous man; he might be carrying a dagger beneath his tunic. True, he'd never heard about Simon *actually* killing anyone who was sympathetic to Rome, but some of the Zealots carried a dagger anyway, just so everyone knew that their political sentiments were sincere. And the Zealots were nothing if not sincere. They were vocal about their hatred for Roman rule and about their hatred for fellow Jews who even contemplated peace with Rome. To them, Romans were an abomination, and anyone who worked with or alongside them was just as bad.

Matthew and the Zealot were enemies. And even though the two of them were as far apart as possible in their huddle, the anger between them was palpable.

Andrew looked at Jesus. They were all waiting for their rabbi to say something. Then, without realizing it, Andrew sighed out loud.

Everyone turned to him. His brother rolled his eyes.

Jesus smiled. "Everything all right, Andrew?"

He shifted his feet and shrugged, unsure of what to say.

The teacher paused to look each of the twelve men in the eye. When Jesus' eyes connected with his own, Andrew found his heart rate slow and his breathing steady. He thought he noticed a bit of sadness in his rabbi's eyes, although it seemed to leave as quickly as it had come.

"My friends," Jesus said, "you are my disciples, and you will be apostles of the Good News that it is time to share. Hear this: You are *all* my disciples. You *all* belong here. Is that understood?"

Andrew nodded his head and looked around the group. The other men were all doing the same.

Jesus nodded as well. "Good."

I huffed onto the couch. "Is it wrong that I want to pray that Eli won't come to small group tonight?"

My friend Meagan rolled her eyes at me. "Yes, Ann, that's awful. God loves Eli and so do we—*right?*"

I cringed. "I *know!* It's just that he's so awkward." I shook my shoulders, already feeling the impending awkwardness. "He's a nice guy, but when he's here we just have to shepherd him through a lot of social awareness stuff and . . . and . . . it's just easier when he's not here." I could feel myself spiraling the longer I talked.

Meagan lifted her eyebrows at me. "Ann. Seriously? I know he can be difficult. But if church isn't a safe place for him, where in the world will he go?"

I pulled my knees up on the couch. "I'm sorry. He's just so hard for me to love."

Maybe you have an Eli in your life—someone who is difficult for you but that you can't get away from. That person might be in your family, in your friendship circle, or in your church. It might be a co-worker, a fellow parent in the PTO, or the coach of your kid's soccer team. Whoever it is, we all have an Eli (or several of them, if we're being honest).

Sometimes these people are difficult because they are unkind or emotionally distant; sometimes it's just because they rub us the wrong way. Being around them steals our sense of peace because we feel off-kilter in their presence.

I can imagine that when Jesus first brought all his disciples together, there was the potential for a *lot* of friction—and a distinct lack of peace. Before Jesus called them, we don't know if the disciples were friends or enemies, if their families had long histories of love or hate. Perhaps Zebedee was in a fight with Thomas's father. Perhaps all the other disciples had snubbed Matthew when they walked by his booth. But regardless of how they interacted before Jesus called them, once he spoke their names, everything changed. They were the original small group. And they didn't get to choose each other.

When Jesus called these disciples to himself, he did so for his own purposes and his own plan. They had absolutely no say about whether they liked the other members. If these disciples wanted to be part of what Jesus was doing on earth, they had to learn to live in community not only with Jesus, but with one another. They had to learn to *be at peace* with Christ and each other.

⸬

This is our call too—to be at peace, even with those who are difficult for us. This does not mean that every hard relationship will suddenly morph into butterflies and rainbows, or that we should ever stay in abusive relationships. What it *does* mean is that, like the disciples, we can learn to have souls that are at rest in the middle of relationships we would never choose on our own—especially with those who are also part of God's family.

> Jesus calls disciples to himself— and to each other—for his own purpose and plan.

Whether our struggle is with a challenging child or a difficult in-law or an annoying small-group member, there is an opportunity for our souls to be at rest when we are with them, because we can trust that God has brought our lives together for his purposes. When we struggle with anxiety over relationships with other believers, we can ask God to help us "accept one another, then, just as Christ accepted you, in order to bring praise to God" (Romans 15:7 NIV). We can ask the Holy Spirit to give us peace as we interact with those who exasperate us—especially with our Elis.

God brings people into and out of our lives for his plans and purposes. Although we will never be able to avoid every difficult relationship, it is possible to learn to be at peace with others as we walk with Christ. Take heart! If a tax collector and a Zealot can go from being enemies to fellow disciples at peace with each other, there is hope for all of us in the challenging relationships in our lives.

- **REFLECT:** God's peace is available to you in your relationships. That's good news! Take some time today and lay any especially challenging relationships before the Lord. Ask him to show you how you can respond to your "Eli" in love—and how your soul can rest in God even as you interact with him or her. The same God who brought the disciples together to change the world is at work in your relationships too!

DAY 27

Peace When Others Leave

"Lord, to whom shall we go? You have the words of eternal life,
and we have believed, and have come to know,
that you are the Holy One of God."

John 6:68

• **Read John 6:60-69** •

Peter felt cold sweat running down his back. *No, no, no.* If only he could get Jesus to just stop talking!

It had been an amazing twenty-four hours. Jesus had fed thousands and thousands of people from just five loaves of barley bread and two measly fish! The food kept reproducing! Once he realized what was happening, Peter's heart rate had kicked up until he felt like he was running the streets rather than handing out lunch. *For once in my life,* Peter thought, *I'm on the right side of things—not with the losers, but with a true leader!* Their miraculous rabbi was gathering a following. *This* was the type of thing that was going to get Jesus to more political and social power— Peter just knew it!

And although none but the twelve had seen it, Jesus had walked on water last night—actually walked *on top of* the waves. If Peter hadn't watched it happen with his own eyes, he never would have believed it. But it *had* happened, and Peter was more convinced than ever that Jesus was God's Anointed One.

But now? Now Jesus was ruining everything! He kept talking about being the "Bread of Life," and the crowd was getting restless. Peter kept making what he hoped were subtle faces at Jesus, willing him to *just stop talking*. Instead, his rabbi raised his voice. "Whoever feeds on my flesh and drinks my blood has eternal life, and I will raise him up on the last day!" The yells from the crowd were full of shock and anger, and Peter sat down. Jesus was ruining their shot at popularity before it had ever really gotten going.

An hour later, when the largest of the crowds had dispersed, Jesus talked with those who considered themselves his disciples—not a small group, by any means, but more intimate than the questioning crowds. "Do you take offense at what I said?" Jesus looked at the group, love and firmness evident in his brown eyes. "The words that I have spoken to you are spirit and life. But there are some of you who do not believe." Many of those looked physically pained by his words; they were fidgeting and squirming where they stood. Jesus sighed deeply. "This is why I told you that no one can come to me unless the Father gives them to me."

Peter watched as most of the other disciples started walking away, shaking their heads. In groups of twos and threes, they turned their backs on Jesus. Peter could tell they wouldn't return.

Twelve of the disciples stood together, and Jesus walked toward them. He looked at them without blinking. "Do you want to go away as well?"

Silence hung in the air until Peter cleared his throat. Their rabbi worked miracles. He healed and fed and walked on water. He was more than a man—he was the Christ! *But why, oh why, does he have to say such strange things? Why does he have to push others away with his words?* Still, there was nowhere else to go.

Peter spoke the truth for the rest of them. "Lord, to whom shall we go? You have the words of eternal life, and we have believed, and have come to know, that you are the Holy One of God."

⁂

One of the most painful things for us after Michael was fired was how friend after friend abandoned us. A gal I had been in small group with—a woman who invited us over for playdates and texted me about life and brought us meals when we were sick—immediately ignored me and pretended I didn't exist. No more texts, no more calls, no more playdates, no more small group. Gone.

Another woman sent me a text to share that God told her she didn't have to be my friend anymore. Others from our church averted their eyes and turned away when they saw me at the grocery store.

These painful friendship hurts (plus too many more to mention) happened between my sisters in Christ and me—not among women who were strangers or unbelievers. They happened with women I had invested in and done ministry with. But what I learned (the hard way) was that the only reason they had befriended me was because of my husband's pastoral position and the assumed power that came with it. Once Michael was fired, the power and prestige didn't exist anymore—and so neither did our friendship.

Those losses made me question myself and my value as a friend, stealing my peace. I was overwhelmed by how hurt I felt, anxious and adrift when it came to friendships.

⁂

As Peter and the other eleven disciples watched Jesus' fame grow through his miracles and public speaking, they also watched his following grow. Jesus had the ability to command huge crowds—thousands upon thousands at a time. And as Jesus became well-known, other men and women decided to follow Jesus too.

But when Jesus starts talking about being the "Bread of Life," and that believers will "eat his flesh and drink his blood," his listeners take offense. The Bible tells us that "many of his disciples turned back and no longer walked with him" (John 6:66).

I can imagine that Jesus grieved their desertion, and also that what happened both angered and hurt the twelve disciples who stayed with him. They believed in him as the Holy One of God—and they didn't want Jesus pushing others away! The dreams they had of his fame (and perhaps their own) disappeared the more he spoke.

> Staying with Jesus—even when friends leave and walk away—is the path of peace.

But Christ has never been apologetic for speaking the truth, even when the truth is hard to hear.

And part of the truth about relationships is this: Some friends *will* leave. They won't like who we are becoming or how we're growing in Christ. Our choices to follow him will make them uncomfortable and they will pull away. It's painful when our friends leave us, but it is an experience that the disciples knew as well. They understood what it was like to see friends walk away from them—and from the Lord.

But the disciples made the right choice when they stayed with Christ. As Peter declared, Jesus has the words of life. He is the Holy One of God! He is the Messiah! Staying with him, even when friends walk away, is the way of abundant life and hope. It is the path of peace.

- **REFLECT:** If you are feeling lonely, or grieving over friends who have left your life, ask the Lord to comfort you. He knows exactly what it means to lose friends. In your pain, he can still give you a soul that is at rest— for as you stay with Christ, you will experience his words of life and the peace that comes from being in relationship with the One who loves you most of all.

DAY 28

Greatness, Humility, and Peace

And he sat down and called the twelve. And he said to them, "If anyone would be first, he must be last of all and servant of all."

Mark 9:35

• **Read Mark 9:33–37** •

Seriously, Bartholomew? In what world do you have *any* claim on being the greatest here?" Thomas rolled his eyes.

Bartholomew repositioned his tunic and kept his eyes on the road ahead. "All I'm saying is that the facts speak for themselves." He glanced at Jesus, who was several paces ahead of the rest of them and out of earshot. They were on their way to Capernaum.

Thomas lobbed the question. "What do you think, Thad? Who's the greatest here?"

Thaddeus, quiet and pensive, waited a beat before responding. "Maybe Peter or James or John." He shrugged. "They're the ones Rabbi always takes with him."

Thad had a point, but Thomas would never concede it out loud. He looked over at Peter, who had a small smirk on his face. James and John kept their heads down, but they were both smiling. Thomas grunted.

Thomas looked around the group. Matthew didn't say anything; he just twirled the gold ring on his right hand around and around. *You're less subtle than you think, man.*

A few hours later, gathered in the home of one of Jesus' family friends, their Master looked around as they were getting ready to settle in for the night.

Jesus' eyes found Thomas. His look was pointed. "What were you discussing on the way here?"

All breath left Thomas's lungs. *He knows.* A stone dropped in his gut. *He knows what we were talking about.* Thomas bent down to re-tie his sandal. *What was I thinking, goading the others with such a question?* Heat flamed to the tips of his ears.

Jesus sat down. "All of you, sit with me." His voice was low. Thomas didn't have to move much; if he could have gotten any lower, he would have.

"If anyone would be first, he must be the last of all—and servant of all." He turned and called to Avner, the youngest son of the family they were lodging with. Little Avner couldn't have been more than three or four years old, and he scampered to Jesus willingly; Thomas had noticed him watching the rabbi from the moment they crossed the threshold. Jesus embraced the boy as his own son; the smile on his face for the little one was the warmest Thomas had ever seen. Thomas found himself envying the boy.

Without prompting, Avner climbed into Jesus' lap and stayed there, his head curled on the rabbi's chest as Jesus continued talking to the twelve.

"Whoever receives a child like this on behalf of me also receives me. And if you receive me, you also receive my Father, who sent me."

Thomas covered his face in shame. The least son in the house was being given a place of honor on Jesus' lap. Rather than lording his authority over this family, their teacher was spending time with the least among them, loving him openly and tenderly—serving him and caring for him.

And I wanted to be the greatest. Thomas's eyes filled with tears. Although his mouth never moved, his heart cried out for forgiveness for his pride. When he looked up, Jesus was already smiling at him.

My stress since Michael's firing was eating into our marriage like a cancer. "Why do I feel like I'm the one who has to carry the weight of this family?"

"You don't, Ann. Only God can carry—"

"But I do!" My anger was hot, and I shot back more quickly than I'd expected. "When you were in seminary for three years, who worked to keep this family going?" I used both hands to point at myself. "Me! And I've carried the anxiety and worry that comes with that!"

Michael shook his head. "The burden doesn't rest on your shoulders."

"But it does!" I pushed out a heavy breath. "Since you've been out of work, who's been keeping this family afloat?" I pointed at myself again, but before I could say anything, Michael practically roared.

"God, Ann! *God* has been taking care of us!" Michael stood up from the table, where we were going over numbers and old wounds. "He's *always* been the one providing for us. I am thankful you work, but you are *not* this family's provider." He exhaled. "And neither am I."

"But I *want* you to be!" I felt the tension in my shoulders and swung my head back to look at the ceiling. My voice quieted, and I said the same thing I'd been saying for years. "I don't want to carry this burden. I'm exhausted by it."

Michael shook his head. "I am too." He sat back down and looked at the space on the table between us. "The burden isn't yours to carry, Ann.

But I can't take it from you. This isn't something I can fix. You have to give it to the Lord."

———※———

When the disciples were arguing about who was the greatest, doubtless they assumed that Jesus couldn't hear them, because as soon as he brought it up, they were shamed to silence. As soon as they were confronted by the Lord, they knew that arguing about greatness in front of him—the Holy One of God—was completely ridiculous. *He* was the greatest, and he was showing them that *service* was the way to be first. They'd had it all wrong.

The Lord alone is the greatest. He alone is the King.

It was the same for me at the kitchen table with my husband. The sinful part of my heart wanted to reiterate to Michael that *I* was doing the heavy lifting in our family by working when he wasn't employed—and because of that, *I* was entitled to more stress, more worry, and more exhaustion. I was short-tempered and easily angered in those days, and I wanted him to give me a pass on my anxiety and stress because of the role I was playing in our family.

I wanted to prove that my "greatness" of working gave me the right to be stressed out and frustrated.

And like the disciples, I soon found myself humbled in the Lord's presence. Because it is true—God is and always has been the one who has provided for our family. He is the source of all provision (Matthew 6:33; 7:9–11), and when I emotionally took on the role of being the sole provider for our family, it was both unbiblical and prideful. *As if I could usurp the God of the universe in his role of being the truest, greatest provider?*

Jesus alone is the greatest. He is the greatest in service, in love, in provision, in care, in kindness, in justice, in mercy. He alone is the King.

If you find yourself anxious and overwhelmed today by something in your life such as power, money, relationships, or work, it might be because you have taken on an emotional role that you were never meant to carry. It's easy for us to see ourselves as the greatest—the most important one in the room—and to forget that we are completely dependent upon the Lord.

Take your anxiety to him today and repent for any way in which you have seen yourself as greater than you are. There is peace in knowing that God is the great one, and that as his children, we are safe in his arms. Like a child in his lap, curled on his chest, we can be at peace in his presence without having anything to offer him.

• **REFLECT:** If the disciples, who lived with Jesus, could argue about being the greatest, surely all of us have areas in our lives where we think we are better than we are. What might that be in your life today? Read Romans 12:3 and ask God to cleanse your heart of false greatness, and then trust that he is ready to embrace you and offer you his peace.

DAY 29

Forgiving Others with Peace in Our Hearts

*Then Peter came to him and asked, "Lord, how often should
I forgive someone who sins against me? Seven times?"
"No, not seven times," Jesus replied, "but seventy times seven!"*
Matthew 18:21–22 NLT

• **Read Matthew 18:21–35** •

Peter tried to unclench his jaw but found he couldn't. Jesus' words stung. "If your brother sins against you, go and tell him his fault, between you and him alone. If he listens to you, you have gained your brother."

After hearing his rabbi's teaching, Peter's mind flitted back to earlier in the day. His insides roiled.

That morning, Matthew and Simon had been arguing again. It was the same old argument, over and over—Matthew explaining his decision to work for the Romans as a tax collector, Simon bellowing back at him for being a traitor to his own people.

Peter had turned to James. "They're both crazy, I think."

James lifted an eyebrow. "Simon's the crazy one. He won't let it go, and it's not like Matthew's at his booth anymore, anyway. We all left our work to follow Jesus."

Peter was surprised. "What? It's Matthew who's the real problem. He sold us out—*his own people*—to gain some coin from our enemies! How in the world can you think Simon's the problem? Sure, he's a Zealot, but at least he's on the right side!"

"The right side?" James scoffed. "I think we should all be pretty clear by now that even our own people aren't on *our side*." He shrugged. "They leave Jesus just as quickly as they flock to him. Our rabbi is a man to himself." He nodded to Jesus, just a stone's throw away. "We don't have sides anymore unless it's with him."

"That's not true!" Peter found himself on his feet, anger rippling through him like a wave. "Jesus is here for *our* people! For once in our lives, we have some hope! How dare you say he's not on our side!"

James's words were almost impossible to hear over the blood thrumming in Peter's ears. "You're wrong, man."

"No, I'm not!" Peter nearly screamed the words, drawing the attention of the rest of their group.

He had stormed away after that, trying to cool off but failing. Now, listening to Jesus teach, he knew he must forgive James for their fight, just as he must ask forgiveness from him. But that drew a question to his heart. Was there a limit on forgiveness? A certain number of times he must forgive before he could hold on to a grudge?

Peter approached Jesus. "Lord, how often will my brother sin against me and I forgive him? As many as seven times?" He felt generous even as he offered the option; most other rabbis said that a limit of forgiving someone three times was what was necessary.[1] This was over double the norm!

1. Douglas Sean O'Donnell notes in his commentary on Matthew in the Preaching the Word series that most Jewish rabbis chose this number based on Amos chapters 1

Jesus looked at Peter and raised an eyebrow, nodding toward James and the other disciples. "No, not seven times, Peter." Jesus shook his head, the hint of a smile on his lips. "Not seven times, but seventy times seven!"

Peter nearly stumbled, he was so taken aback. What Jesus was saying meant that there was *no end* to forgiving a brother.

───※───

Betsy was yet another woman from our church who had dropped off the face of the earth when Michael lost his pastoral position. As with most people from church, I worried about seeing her again in public. I was nervous about finding myself caught in a situation where I might have to act like everything was fine between us when it wasn't.

Out of the blue one day, she texted me to see if we could get lunch together. I agreed but felt nauseated every time I thought about it in the days leading up to our meeting. What in the world was I going to say? What was *she* going to say? Having ignored us during some of the hardest months of our lives, she no longer felt like a safe person; I wasn't going to open up and share the deep parts of my heart with her as I had before.

Additionally, I didn't know if she wanted to get together and pretend like the last three months hadn't happened, or if she wanted to apologize. I prayed and prayed, asking God to calm my heart and help me handle the conversation well.

No matter what she said or didn't say, I felt that I needed to come to the meeting with forgiveness in my heart.

At our lunch meeting, I was nervous. I knew I had done the internal and spiritual work with the Lord ahead of time, but my palms were sweaty under the table; I picked at my food.

───────

and 2. (Douglas Sean O'Donnell, *Matthew: All Authority in Heaven and on Earth*, Series Ed. Kent Hughes [Wheaton, IL: Crossway, 201], 521.)

We spent the first hour of lunch making small talk. Betsy seemed perfectly comfortable shooting the breeze; internally, I was a mess.

Just when I was about to say I needed to leave, she spoke abruptly.

"I—I know that I haven't reached out for a while. I thought so many times about how much you must have needed a friend, and how I should've reached out to you. But I didn't. I'm sorry."

I looked away, unable to hold her gaze. "I did need a friend." One deep breath. "Almost everyone has walked away from us, and it's been lonely."

Betsy nodded. She didn't offer any explanation, didn't say anything else.

I sat there, struggling against what I knew I needed to say and what I knew I needed to offer to her. The sounds of people at the tables around us softened the silence as I pleaded internally with the Lord—again—to help me forgive her. It was harder with her in front of me than it had been in the prayer closet.

I turned to Betsy, speaking the words that were so hard but so needed for both of us. "I forgive you."

I was able to leave our lunch with a peace I hadn't felt before—not because our friendship was suddenly healed, but because I had released Betsy from the burden of having to fix how she had hurt me.

In the weeks that followed, I realized that I no longer harbored anxiety about seeing her again or about our next conversation. While our friendship would never be the same, I had forgiven her, and my soul was able to be at peace, knowing that God was in control. I had done my part by extending forgiveness to her; the rest was up to him.

⸻

What Jesus told Peter was radical: that forgiving others was not about a quota to be met, but about a posture of the heart. Jesus knew what Peter could not yet fully understand—that all sins against others are ultimately sins against God. Jesus also knew that through his death and resurrection, he would pay for those sins for all time.

But on that day when he asked Jesus what the "forgiveness limit" was, I don't think Peter was looking for an answer from Jesus that required a change of heart. I think Peter just wanted to be right. He wanted to know how long he had to put up with someone else's sin before he could write them off entirely.

Thankfully, Christ's response was better than Peter's question, for Christ calls us to be people who forgive consistently and without measure. We are called to mimic Jesus' way of forgiving, which is grounded not in the offense done against us, but in the God who forgives us first.

> **Forgiveness is grounded not in the offense done against us, but in the God who forgives us first.**

But it is hard—*so hard*—to forgive those who hurt us. We can only do it when we have God's help to forgive . . . and when we remember that we are also in need of constant forgiveness.

In *any* relationship in our lives, forgiveness will be needed if we are going to live in peace. Without it, our relationships will be full of anger and bitterness. So if you are struggling to forgive someone who has hurt you today, the good news is that the Lord wants to help you forgive them. While we cannot muster up forgiveness on our own, we can ask God to give us a heart that is *willing* to forgive. We can ask him to help us forgive those who have hurt us, and ask him to help us look to Christ as the one who has taken all hurt and sin for us already.

Then we will be able to forgive "seventy times seven"—not 490 times, but as many times at it takes.

- **REFLECT:** Who do you need to forgive today? Ask the Lord to help you release that person from any anger or bitterness you hold against them, and to give you a heart that is willing to let go of offense. He will help you as you continue to ask him to do this.

DAY 30

Peace between Those
Who Are Offended

*For even the Son of Man came not to be served but to serve,
and to give his life as a ransom for many.*

Mark 10:45

• **Read Mark 10:35–45** •

*S*eriously? Peter was fuming. *How dare James and John ask for places of honor!* He'd just heard what the brothers had asked Jesus and was taking a walk to clear his head. Instead, he was getting angrier.

How much better than everyone else must James and John think they were to ask to sit at the right and left hand of Jesus when he came into his kingdom? Peter was incredulous. *The nerve of those men!* It wasn't like they were the only ones Jesus had singled out for special privileges—Peter had been with them every single time Jesus had pulled them aside! And it was Peter who had gotten a new name from Jesus—not James and John. Yes, the Lord had changed *his* name from Simon to Peter when he'd finally said out loud what he knew in his bones—that Jesus really was the Messiah, the Son of God.

If anyone has a right to ask for a place of honor, it's me. Peter stormed back to the rest of the disciples and found James and John apart from the other nine. The others were purposefully ignoring them.

Peter blew a huff of air through his nose. *Serves them right.*

They all straightened wordlessly as Jesus walked toward them.

"Come here, my brothers." The twelve gathered to stand in the circle they often formed around their rabbi. As he spoke, he looked at each of them. "You know that those who are considered rulers of the Gentiles lord it over them, and their great ones exercise authority over them."

Peter nodded. Everyone knew that. But what did this have to do with the chastisement that James and John surely needed?

"But it shall not be so among you. Whoever would be great among you must be your servant, and whoever would be first among you must be slave of all." Jesus looked up to the heavens before talking again. "For even the Son of Man came not to be served but to serve, and to give his life as a ransom for many."

One by one, the men in their circle nodded at Jesus and sent sideways glances to James and John, who both appeared repentant. They would all be hugging by nightfall. But Peter couldn't do it—not yet.

He wanted to be great! More than many other things, Peter yearned for greatness. But here was his Lord, telling him that greatness wouldn't come from power and position, but from service.

Ugh. If he was honest with himself, Peter was angry that James and John had thought to ask Jesus the question before he had. He wanted a place by his Lord forever, and felt that out of all of them, he was most entitled to it.

His eyes widened as he felt his own pride like a physical blow on his chest. How could he be entitled to anything if even Jesus came to serve? He ducked his head, his pride melting away—along with his anger at James and John. *Lord, help me,* Peter thought. *Help me want to serve more than I long for power. Help me be truly great.*

※

Has anyone ever offended you?

Years ago, when we were at a different church, I was helping to organize the yearly women's retreat. We prayed through and talked about every detail: the theme, location, food, decorations, and speaker. I loved speaking at women's events and conferences, and I hoped that my own church would ask me to speak at this retreat.

During one of our planning meetings, the possibility of my being the speaker was discussed, and I was thrilled when everyone seemed excited about it. But a couple weeks later, the team decided to ask someone else from our congregation to speak.

While I knew I wasn't the only choice for a speaker at this retreat, my initial response was to feel hurt. Over the next few days, that hurt blossomed into anger and then into offense. *Who did they think they were, choosing this other woman over me? She was younger! And less experienced!*

As I prayed about everything swirling in my heart, the Lord showed me that what was underneath all my hurt and anger was actually spiritual pride. I was hurt because I felt rejected—an understandable emotion. But I was angry because I felt *entitled;* I thought I was great and that my spiritual greatness should be rewarded with an invitation to speak. And I saw myself as more spiritually mature than the woman they invited to speak. As the Holy Spirit pulled back the ugliness of my sin, I could see with awful clarity that I thought I was better than her.

James and John were asking for something similar—power and position based on their own perceived spiritual standing. As those close to Jesus, they felt they deserved places of honor next to him, showing their own spiritual pride. And when the other disciples heard about their conversation, they became offended at these brothers—because of *their* own spiritual pride.

Any time we find ourselves thinking, "How dare they!" or, "Who do they think they are?" it's a flashing light for us to look into the mirror and reconsider who we really think *we* are. Offense with others often comes from seeing ourselves as more important than we are—something the Scriptures caution us against: "I say to everyone among you not to think of himself more highly than he ought to think, but to think with sober judgment, each according to the measure of faith that God has assigned" (Romans 12:3).

When we are able to see ourselves truly and rightly—as desperate sinners in need of a savior—the offense that we feel toward others will melt away. They need grace and forgiveness for their sin just as we need grace and forgiveness for our own sin. There is no hierarchy in God's kingdom other than the one where Jesus is King and the rest of us are equal at the foot of the cross.

Jesus brings peace between those who are offended, because he asks us to look at him as our standard, rather than at each other. In light of who Christ is, every single one of us falls short. We have no reason to be prideful—and no reason to be resentful—when we consider that every sin against us is ultimately a sin against Jesus, and that every way others fall short is not about how they fail us, but about how they ultimately fail Christ.

Peace comes when we acknowledge and repent of our own spiritual pride so that we can approach God and others with humility through service. That is the place of true greatness.

> **Jesus brings peace between those who are offended, because he asks us to look at him as our standard, rather than at each other.**

- **REFLECT:** Where might you need to repent from spiritual pride and offense today? Ask the Lord to help you see yourself rightly—as a sinner saved by grace and not by your own goodness. Then find peace in knowing that you are loved and cherished by the One who saved you.

SECTION 7

· · ·

MARY MAGDALENE

Peace in Letting Go

DAYS 31–35

DAY 31

The Peace that Freedom Brings

*And the twelve were with him, and also some women who
had been healed of evil spirits and infirmities: Mary, called
Magdalene, from whom seven demons had gone out . . .*

Luke 8:1–2

• Read Luke 8:1-2 •

Mary Magdalene looked at the group surrounding Jesus, noting that several of the men, including the rabbi, would need new tunics before the month's end. Their travel was constant, and their clothes took a beating. She rubbed her right knee under her dress and repositioned her scarf. How thankful she was to sit and listen to their rabbi and learn from him—all while letting her knees rest.

She was not used to traveling like this, although she counted it the highest privilege of her life to follow Jesus as a disciple. To be fair, she was not used to anything like what she had known for these past months: peace.

True peace.

For years piled upon years—so many years she had lost track of them—her life had been swathed in darkness. She didn't know when the first torment started, although she remembered being young. She couldn't have been more than nine or ten years old when that bottomless fear began to wake her in the night, full of hellish impressions that ran through her mind with the speed of a stallion.

The things she saw in her dreams made her afraid, and that fear spilled over into her waking hours as a horror she could not escape. Her mind would run in different directions, causing her speech to slur and her eyes to dart unendingly. She was terrified of everything she saw, of everything she felt. Sometimes her very skin seemed to try and slither away from her, and she felt her body was being torn in different directions. She could not stop the screaming that rose out of her like an animal. She could not stop any of it.

Years puddled into one another like drops in an endless ocean of terror, and by the time she was in her twenties, she was alone. Her days and nights blurred. She rarely slept. Her hair tangled around her. Her muscles cramped with pain and disuse. How long had she lived like this? Was she even living anymore?

And then, months ago, there had been a man at the door of her house. He was bathed in a light she could feel rather than see, and it drew her and frightened her all at once.

The words he said were simple: "Foul spirits, come out of her."

Like the pulling a stopper from an upended bottle of wine, she felt each presence of darkness drip out of her body in steady succession. *One, two, three* . . . already she could hear more clearly and see with greater precision. *Four, five* . . . she felt her mind still and settle. *Six.* Her hands stopped their trembling. *Seven.* She knew herself again, as Mary.

The man in front of her smiled, his brown eyes warm with acceptance and kindness. "Mary of Magdala, you are free. Come, follow me."

Mary Magdalene felt a familiar wetness on her cheeks and wiped the tears gently away. Jesus of Nazareth was the man who had freed her. He was the man who had given her the peace she craved every day of her long torment. She had walked out of her house that day and never looked back, choosing to follow him wholeheartedly.

Now she listened to Jesus talking about the kingdom of God and the cost of following him, and she knew that whatever the cost of being his disciple, she would pay it gladly.

※

Not much is known about Mary of Magdala—or Mary Magdalene, as she is often called. The Scriptures are scant on their details about her life before meeting Jesus, although there is no question that she was a woman whom Christ had set free. The Bible references multiple times when Jesus freed people of demonic oppression, and yet here, in Luke 8, the gospel takes special note that there were a handful of women who helped support Jesus in his ministry—women whom he had freed from "evil spirits" and "infirmities." Mary Magdalene is unique in this list as one who had suffered from "evil spirits" that were extreme: Luke clarifies that she was freed from seven demons. Her torment must have been severe; her pain and isolation unbearable.

And yet, even in her acute state, she was not too far from Jesus' saving power. He has *all* power, and the Bible is clear in showing that every demon he cast out had to immediately obey (see Mark 5:1–13 and Mark 9:14–29 for two examples). His encounter with Mary, although not recorded, would not have been any different: Every evil spirit obeys Jesus, as king of the universe. When he freed Mary Magdalene, she was *truly* free from the demons that tormented her. For the first time in her life, Mary experienced real peace.

It's unsurprising, then, that she became one of the most loyal disciples that Jesus had. She followed him, helped to provide for his material needs, and stayed with him until the bitter end of his death on the cross (see Mark 15:40–47).

Mary's previous bondage to evil never kept her from faithfully following Jesus. In fact, the unspoken implication of her life is that the peace and freedom Christ offered meant so much to her that she funneled that gratitude into worship, obedience, and love.

> No one has too much fear or anxiety for Jesus to replace with his peace.

The example of Mary Magdalene's love for and obedience to Jesus is one for us to follow, for each of us have been given true freedom and peace in Christ. Perhaps you were not freed of seven demons, but if Christ has saved and redeemed you, you *have* been freed. You *have* been given the peace that comes from belonging to him, rather than belonging to darkness: "He has delivered us from the domain of darkness and transferred us to the kingdom of his beloved Son, in whom we have redemption, the forgiveness of sins" (Colossians 1:13–14).

No one is too deep in darkness for Jesus to save. No one is in too much bondage for Jesus to set free. No one is too overwhelmed to receive Jesus' comfort. No one has too much fear that Jesus can't replace it with his peace. If he can save and redeem Mary Magdalene, giving her the freedom and peace that she so desperately needed, he can do the same for you, *right now*. He is the King of all—and he will help you today.

• **REFLECT:** If you are a believer in Jesus, the same Lord who freed Mary Magdalene is your Lord too. If you carry places inside that feel broken or oppressed by darkness or bondage, ask Christ to come and free you

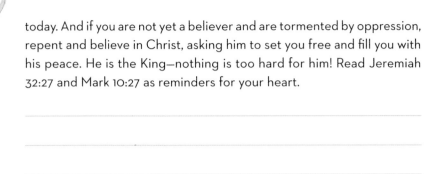

today. And if you are not yet a believer and are tormented by oppression, repent and believe in Christ, asking him to set you free and fill you with his peace. He is the King—nothing is too hard for him! Read Jeremiah 32:27 and Mark 10:27 as reminders for your heart.

DAY 32

Peace in Relinquishing Our Dreams

There were also many women there, looking on from a distance,
who had followed Jesus from Galilee, ministering to him, among
whom were Mary Magdalene and Mary the mother of James
and Joseph and the mother of the sons of Zebedee.

Matthew 27:55–56

• **Read Matthew 27:45-56** •

The shock of Jesus' last day had left Mary Magdalene without any tears left to shed; now all she felt was the hollowness of loss gaping like a cavern between her ribs.

Jesus was gone. And it had happened so quickly! Just a week ago the crowds had been cheering him in the streets as he rode on the back of a donkey. Now? She looked toward Golgotha and could see his body still hanging from the nails that held him to the cross, limp as a rag doll. His death had been worse than anything she could have imagined; at every turn, there had been betrayal and lies, cover-ups and cowardice.

Salome—her dear friend and the mother of James and John—was weeping in her arms, nearly unmoving. They had been closer to his cross earlier in the day, but as the crowds grew restless and angrier, the women had been pushed from his side. Mary Magdalene didn't know what was worse—to be near him and see his agony up close, or to be too far away to see his eyes.

It didn't matter now. Her Lord, her rabbi—the one who had freed her and offered her the peace she had never experienced before—was dead.

For Salome's sake, Mary Magdalene sucked in a pocketful of air and whispered into her friend's ear, "We must get you away from here, Salome. Let us go." Salome nodded but made no effort to move.

Mary pulled herself up from the ground with legs that felt like limestone. She saw some of the other women from their group and led Salome to them. Every single woman had red-rimmed eyes that looked as if they had lost all hope.

They had.

After handing off Salome, Mary Magdalene turned back toward the cross. Even now, she could not bear to leave Jesus' side.

But she had to sit; her body was unable to carry her further. Her eyes found Jesus' form still hanging on the cross. All she had known since he freed her from her torment was following him as his disciple. There had only been darkness and agony before him; being in his presence was light and life and peace. Her only dream was to keep following him forever. What would she do now? Where would she go?

The tears came, slow but unrelenting. Mary Magdalene had no life apart from the band of disciples; she had no community apart from them, no purpose. The months she had spent with Jesus had been the best of her life, and for the first time in her memory, she had felt hopeful and peaceful. She had even been excited about her future—because she didn't worry about what was ahead, as long as she could follow Jesus. Now he was gone, and all her dreams with him.

How could she move forward? What was she going to do?

All of us have had moments in life where we have experienced the death of a dream. It might have been the crushing of a professional dream, or the loss of a dream for our future. Perhaps the person we loved passed into eternity, or the plans we had for our lives fell apart. Maybe the opportunity we were promised never materialized, or the friendship we relied on disappointed us. Whatever it is, the death of a dream often stuns and confuses us. It leaves us overwhelmed and unsure about how to move forward in life.

I grew up as part of the fourth generation in our family home, and my dream was always to put down roots and raise a family in one place forever. Sure, I wanted to travel and see the world—but always with the safety of returning to a home where we were settled and secure. That had been my childhood, and I loved it; I could think of no better experience for my own kids.

That dream has died multiple times. When my daughter was two years old, we moved so that my husband could pursue seminary. When she was three and a half, we moved to be near family because of my depression borne out of multiple miscarriages. When she was five, we moved across the country for my husband's new pastoral position, and when she was six and a half we moved yet again after Michael was fired and God provided a new job. Four moves in less than five years. I came to hate moving boxes.

Every time we moved, I found myself wrestling with the death of my dream of stability. I wanted to stay put; all we seemed to do was move. No, our moves weren't life-shattering. But they were emotionally draining and relationally devastating. My peace felt paper-thin with every transition; every year and a half, I wondered how I would start over again. I often felt overwhelmed, lonely, and adrift. Aside from figuring out new doctors and grocery stores and libraries, the deeper questions tugged at me: How do I make and trust new friends once again? Where do I fit? Where do I belong?

The loss of the dream of stability wasn't my only dream, but it's one I've had to die to over and over again. And every time felt like a significant loss.

But Mary Magdalene truly believed she had lost *everything* on that day at the cross. All the hope that she had for the future was tied up in the person of Jesus Christ—the one who had saved her and given her hope. When he died, surely she felt that all she had ever hoped for died with him.

What Mary didn't know was that just around the corner, Christ would defeat death with blazing glory. But even then, she would have to let go of the dream she had for her life. Most likely, what she wanted forever was to continue to follow Jesus in the flesh, learning and growing as his disciple along with the others who followed him. Who could conceive of anything more glorious?

For when Jesus did return, it was not as she might have hoped. His promise was that he would always be with his disciples, but no longer in the flesh. There would be no more traveling around Israel, no more preaching on the mountainside, no more feeding the thousands with a handful of bread and fish. Instead, the gift of his Holy Spirit was Christ's promise that he would be with them in their hearts, but not in body (see John 14:16–17).

Mary Magdalene had to relinquish the dream that she had for her life *as she had known it* in order to embrace the new life Jesus was offering to her as a disciple: one not of flesh and blood, but of spirit and truth (see John 4:24). Jesus himself said

> Relinquishing our dreams to Christ leads to peace in him.

that it was better for his disciples to have the indwelling Holy Spirit than to him in person:

> "Nevertheless, I tell you the truth: it is to your advantage that I go away, for if I do not go away, the Helper will not come to you. But if I go, I will send him to you. And when he comes, he will convict the world concerning sin and righteousness and judgment" (John 16:7–8).

The gift of the Holy Spirit would be the greatest gift any believer could have—the presence of Christ with them at all times! But it might not have seemed that way at first. The loss of the physical presence of Jesus would have felt painful and hard. Mary Magdalene, like all the disciples, would have had to relinquish her dream of life with Christ *as she knew it* in order to accept life with Christ *as he would give it*—in the way that is best.

Whenever we have to relinquish our dreams to Jesus and let go of what we want, there will be sorrow. But on the other side of that relinquishing is the peace and comfort that comes from accepting the Lord's plans for us, and having a soul that is at rest in the midst of circumstances we didn't choose.

Although I never wanted to move so many times, the Lord has used our nomadic journey to shift my concept of stability from a physical place to a spiritual reality: I know now, in a way I did not know beforehand, that my security is in Christ, no matter where I lay my head. The dream that died in my life has led me to the better reality of knowing Jesus as my security in all things.

If there is a dream you need to relinquish to the Lord today, take heart. Whatever you may lose here on earth, painful though it may be, is an opportunity to find peace in Christ's provision, presence, and plan for you. His dreams for us are better than our own.

- **REFLECT:** Pray this prayer with me today: Lord, help me to trust you when I experience the death of a dream in my life. You have plans for me that I don't fully understand, and I ask for your peace today as I choose to believe that what you give me is even better than my dreams for myself.

DAY 33

Peace through Service

And Joseph bought a linen shroud, and taking him down,
wrapped him in the linen shroud and laid him in a tomb
that had been cut out of the rock. And he rolled a stone against
the entrance of the tomb. Mary Magdalene and Mary
the mother of Joses saw where he was laid.

Mark 15:46–47

• **Read Luke 23:50-56; Mark 15:46-47** •

Mary Magdalene inched her way closer to the cross with one of the other women; they were waiting to see what would be done with Jesus' body. According to tradition, he should be prepared for burial. But time was growing short: sundown was near, and with it came the Sabbath. They could do no work on the Sabbath, not even to care for his body. Anxiety tightened her throat with fear. Her Lord was still hanging there, his blood beginning to dry on his precious face and feet. She felt so helpless! As a woman, she had no recourse, no way to make sure he was given the proper burial he so deeply deserved. So she prayed, not knowing what else to do.

The sun was already in the final third of the sky. Mary bit her lip. *He cannot hang there all night! It would be an abomination!*

Movement to her right caught her attention, and she watched two men making their way, steadily and purposefully, toward his cross. She did not know them, but they looked important—well-dressed men who carried authority. They approached the guards and, after a few moments of talking, apparently were granted permission to go nearer to Jesus' body.

Mary Magdalene's heart was frantic. *What are they going to do? My Lord must be respected, his body properly prepared for burial!* She watched. They were going to take his body. And—*oh!*—they were being so gentle. *Perhaps these men love Jesus too?* Tears clouded her vision as she noted the kindness and tenderness with which they removed him from that horrible cross.

The men carried Jesus like a child between them, and Mary squeezed her friend's hand. "We must follow them. We must know where they place our Lord."

They walked behind the men at a distance. When they reached a garden nearby, the two men carefully laid Jesus down inside a tomb and began hasty preparations, wrapping his body in a linen shroud with spices. Night was chasing the daylight; they were running out of time. Mary could smell the myrrh from where she waited across from the tomb, but their work was too quick. She didn't begrudge the men, but she had seen she had to do more—had to see Jesus buried properly. If her Lord could not live, she would serve him even in his death.

Mary Magdalene knew her purpose, at least for the next days. Now that she knew where they had laid Jesus' body, she would come back and give him the burial he ought to have, with the appropriate washing and anointing their customs required.

As soon as the men rolled the stone across the tomb's entrance, she grabbed her friend's hand and flew. She needed to spend the rest of the daylight preparing spices and ointments for her Lord.

⁓

Mary Magdalene's life became very small and narrow in a matter of hours: Her entire existence as she knew it was over.

Jesus was gone and she didn't yet know that he would be coming back to defeat death. But what she did know was that he deserved a burial worthy of a man of honor, and she was determined to give that to him. And so, even in her grief and pain, Mary Magdalene and her friend decided that they would do what they could to tangibly serve Jesus in the middle of their own sorrow. Now Mary had a reason to keep going.

> Serving Jesus with others, even in our pain, offers us purpose— and often, peace.

This model that Mary offers us here in this small moment in the Scriptures is something both beautiful and profound: Serving Jesus with others, even in our pain, offers us purpose and peace.

I have experienced this truth in the midst of my own sorrow multiple times, although at first, I didn't live it out well. In my grief after our miscarriages, I tended toward isolation. I was rightly heartbroken, and my sorrow was deep. But instead of finding ways to envelop myself in my church community and with friends, I pulled away. I wasn't sure how to handle my sadness around others, and I didn't want to feel any more vulnerable. What I didn't know was that my choice to isolate myself brought about even more pain and sadness—much of which could have been avoided if I had reached out rather than pulling away.

Mary Magdalene shows us that grief and community—and sadness and service—are not mutually exclusive. Instead, Mary serves Jesus *in* her grief, alongside others. I can imagine that as she and her friend prepared burial spices, they wept together. The ointments that they fashioned would have been sprinkled with their own tears. Perhaps they talked about Jesus and his words even as they mixed and crushed and stirred. But those very actions of talking about him, remembering him, and crying together were the gateway to healing and peace.

When I was hurting after Michael's job loss, I realized I needed to serve, even in my own sorrow. It was a tender time; I did nothing huge and offered no grand gestures. But I did choose small ways to serve. I coordinated teacher appreciation events at our daughter's school, forcing myself to remember and appreciate others who were working hard to love our children. I organized a simple fundraiser for a friend who was adopting a child. And I refused to isolate myself. We visited a small group at the new church we started attending, choosing to engage with Christ's people. These were not grandiose, ongoing acts of service or community—I did not have the emotional energy to start a new ministry or make a bunch of new friends. But I did what I could, and I reached *out* rather than spiraling *in*.

It made a world of difference in my heart and spirit. For as I served Christ by serving others, even in those small ways, my sorrow was met with peace. My soul began to rest as I was able to see, with fresh eyes, that there were many others in the body of Christ who loved us and were helping us—and that I could help them too.

The Bible highlights this truth for us:

Blessed be the God and Father of our Lord Jesus Christ, the Father of mercies and God of all comfort, who comforts us in all our affliction, so that we may be able to comfort those who are in any affliction, with the comfort with which we ourselves are comforted by God.

2 Corinthians 1:3–4

As we serve others, even in the midst of our own trials, we will find ourselves enveloped in the comfort of God and upheld by the peace of God. This does not mean that we *must* serve in order to experience his comfort and peace—not at all. There are some seasons where we need to acknowledge that we cannot and should not serve; rather, we need to allow the body of Christ to serve us.

But when we are able to do so, the beautiful reality of the kingdom of God is that serving others out of our own pain actually helps to heal that pain. Ministering to others in our own struggle actually helps bring peace to that struggle. For when we serve Christ's people, we are serving Christ. As our Lord comforts us, we can then comfort others, and they, in turn, can help to comfort us again. It is the body of Christ healing itself through the presence of Jesus; it is his peace at work in and through people.

- **REFLECT:** Where can you serve right now? Even if you are in a season of sorrow, ask the Lord to help you serve others in small ways. For as we attend to the needs of others, our attention is wonderfully drawn away from our own pain to the condition of others—and to Christ's presence and peace in our midst.

_____

_____

_____

DAY 34

Peace through the Resurrection

Jesus said to her, "Woman, why are you weeping? Whom are you seeking?" Supposing him to be the gardener, she said to him, "Sir, if you have carried him away, tell me where you have laid him, and I will take him away." Jesus said to her, "Mary." She turned and said to him in Aramaic, "Rabboni!" (which means Teacher).

John 20:15–16

• **Read John 20:1–16** •

Mary Magdelene shoved her palms to her eyes, willing herself to stop crying. She needed to think. Peter and John had already come and gone, both of them just as confused as she was about the disappearance of Jesus' body. Where could her Lord have gone? Who could have taken him?

This was all she had left to do for him—to prepare his body, rightly, for burial. She had spent the Sabbath mentally ticking every box of preparation since she could do nothing with her hands, and then had gotten up early this morning with the other women to purchase the rest of the burial spices they needed. But when they had arrived, the stone—which they had worried about being able to move because it was so heavy—was already rolled to the side. There was no body inside and no guards remained. Mary panicked and ran to Peter and John, who came and left. The other women had left as well. But Mary could not will herself to leave the tomb. This was the last place Jesus had been, and she didn't know where to go or what to do. So she stood in front of the empty tomb and let her tears fall.

Her sorrow dropped her to her knees, and she looked into the tomb as she did so. Her eyes widened when she saw two men, blazing like the whitest fire. They sat on the slab where Jesus had been.

"Woman, why are you weeping?"

Between her tears and shock, Mary Magdalene could barely find her voice. "They—they have taken away my Lord and I do not know where they have laid him."

She heard a noise behind her and turned to see a man silhouetted by the sun behind him. He repeated the same question to her. "Woman, why are you weeping?" His voice was kind. "Whom are you seeking?"

Perhaps he is the gardener! "Sir, if you have carried him away, tell me where you have laid him and I will take him away."

Her eyes adjusted to the light, and she found herself looking at a face that felt familiar. Then he smiled at her. "Mary."

She gasped as her heart leapt in surprise and wonder. "Rabboni!"

⁂

Have you ever seen a loved one that you didn't expect to see—perhaps out of context or at an unexpected time or place? I'll never forget the afternoon when my dad came to visit me unexpectedly. I was in college, having a hard semester. It had been a particularly difficult week, and then, all of a sudden, he was on campus. He hadn't told me he was making the trip or that he was on his way. But he appeared outside of my dorm to encircle me in a hug.

I remember the relief and comfort that I felt in his presence; this was my father, the man who loved me and cared about me. With him, I didn't have to pretend that everything was okay or keep it all together. I could let my guard down and share my heart with him.

And that's exactly what I did. He had heard the strain in my voice over the phone the night before and read me like a book. While he couldn't stay long, he drove up to the Chicago suburbs to hug me, take me out to dinner, listen to me process life, and remind me that I was loved. The gift of being with him on that Wednesday afternoon, when I least expected to see him, is a memory I'll treasure forever.

Mary Magdalene surely did not expect to see Jesus standing on his feet that Sunday morning. She had watched as his lifeblood poured out of him in ribbons of red just days before; she saw his agony up close. He had *died*. And yet here on this early morning, Jesus was in front of her, speaking her name! She was the first to see the resurrected Christ. Her shock and wonder must have been unmatched.

As the shock subsided, can you imagine the peace that Mary Magdalene would have felt in his presence? Everything wrong was being made right in his very person. For if Jesus was still alive, her hope was not gone! The future she had dreamed of was not lost. Her Lord was still here!

> **Because of Christ's death and resurrection, we now have the peace that his victory brings!**

This is the peace that *only* the resurrection of Jesus can offer to us: the assurance that our hope is not gone, and that everything wrong will be made right through the person of Christ. Because of the sacrificial death of Jesus that paid for our sin, and because of his resurrection, which defeated death, we now have the peace that his victory brings, along with the hope of eternal life with him:

And I heard a loud voice from the throne saying, "Behold, the dwelling place of God is with man. He will dwell with them, and they will be his people, and God himself will be with them as their God. He will wipe away every tear from their eyes, and death shall be no more, neither shall there be mourning, nor crying, nor pain anymore, for the former things have passed away."

And he who was seated on the throne said, "Behold, I am making all things new." (Revelation 21:3–5)

In Christ, there will be no more pain or death or tears. He is making all things new. What Mary Magdalene experienced that early Sunday morning in the person of the resurrected Christ was the first glimpse any human had of the eternal peace and hope that is available to those who believe in him.

Christ has permanently defeated death, pain, and sorrow—forever. Although we will face trials here on earth, a day is coming when those things will be gone and only the goodness and glory of Jesus will exist. Take comfort in this truth! Let your heart be at peace knowing that Christ is making all things—even the dead things—new.

- **REFLECT:** How can the truth and hope of the resurrection shape your life right now? As a believer in Jesus, his eternal peace and hope are yours. Take time to think about Christ's resurrection today. Dwell on the glory that awaits us in his presence eternally, and let that beautiful truth bring peace to whatever you face today.

DAY 35

Peace through Embracing
a New Life

*Jesus said to her, "Do not cling to me, for I have not yet
ascended to the Father; but go to my brothers and say to them,
'I am ascending to my Father and your Father, to my God
and your God.'" Mary Magdalene went and announced to
the disciples, "I have seen the Lord"—and that
he had said these things to her.*

John 20:17–18

● **Read John 20:11–18** ●

It was Jesus! Mary wrapped her arms around his ankles, afraid that if she let go, he might disappear. Her tears were ones of joy now—and her heart was so full she felt she might burst.

Jesus touched her head gently. "Do not cling to me, for I have not yet ascended to the Father; but go to my brothers and say to them, 'I am ascending to my Father and your Father, to my God and your God.'"

217

Mary looked up at him, smiling through her tears. She saw love in his eyes and glory shining from his face. Although she didn't want to let go of her Lord, she also understood that he would not be here long. He was ascending to the Father of all—to God their Father—sometime soon. Yes, Jesus was alive. But things would not be as they were before.

Still, she felt no fear. Here, in his presence, fear did not exist. All she felt was peace: peace and excitement for what his resurrection meant for all of them! No, she did not understand what it all meant yet, but she did realize that the man in front of her was much more than a man. He was the Lord—he was divine!

Mary Magdalene hugged his ankles once again, and then she rose to do as he commanded. She would obey. "Oh, teacher! I am so happy! I will tell the brothers." She ran toward their meeting place, looking back every few steps to see if he was still there. When she looked back a third time, he was gone.

Mary Magdalene bounded into the upper room, where everyone was bent over with sorrow and exhaustion. She didn't wait. "I have seen the Lord!" she yelled. Their heads snapped up, and she continued. "He is alive! As real as you or me. And he told me to tell you this: 'I am ascending to my Father and your Father, to my God and your God.'"

Mary Magdalene was the first person to see the resurrected Christ (see also Mark 16:9). Can you imagine it? The honor of being the first human to see and talk with Jesus after his resurrection was reserved for her alone—a woman who believed him, followed him, loved him, and was committed to him even through and after his death.

And although she undoubtedly wanted to keep clinging to him (who would not?), she was also quick to obey him when he told her to go and share the news of his resurrection with the disciples. Although the men would not believe her right away (see Mark 16:11), the appearance of Jesus among them later in the day confirmed her news. And when Jesus *did* appear to the disciples that evening, his first words to them were, "Peace be with you" (see John 20:19).

After his resurrection and appearance to Mary Magdalene—and the charge he gave her to share the news of his life!—his first words to his followers were words of *peace*. This is why Jesus came: to provide peace for those who follow him. Mary surely felt that peace in his presence outside of the tomb that morning. The disciples felt that peace when he appeared to them that same evening (after their shock wore off). But this peace was not just a feeling—it was the peace that had been won by Jesus through his death and resurrection: the peace that was available with God. Now, every follower of Christ would have peace with God. No more enmity, no more separation due to sin. Sin had been paid for once and for all on the cross, and every believer now was at peace with God the Father—the best news of all time.

Mary Magdalene had the honor of being the first one to announce that this peace had come when she shared the news of the risen Christ with others. It was a role she would continue to carry for the rest of her life, modeling for us what it means to obey Jesus and carry the news of his resurrection to others who need to hear it. And now, it is a role we have the honor of carrying as well: We are those who declare the peace with God that is available through Christ.

> We now have peace with God because of what Christ accomplished on our behalf.

This type of peace means having a soul at rest in God, not only for today, but for all time. If you have never experienced the peace that comes from accepting Christ as your Lord and Savior, his eternal peace is available to you, right now, through the repentance of sin and faith in him. He longs to save you from your sin and give you the promise of eternity with him. Repent and believe the good news of Jesus the Redeemer!

If you already know and love the Lord Jesus, take time today to remember the amazing gift of peace that was won for you through his horrific death and miraculous resurrection. We now have *peace with God* because of what Christ accomplished on our behalf—something we could never gain on our own:

> Therefore, since we have been justified by faith, we have peace with God through our Lord Jesus Christ. Through him we have also obtained access by faith into this grace in which we stand, and we rejoice in hope of the glory of God. (Romans 5:1–2)

- **REFLECT:** What do you need to do today to walk in Christ's peace? Do you need to trust in him, perhaps for the first time? If so, talk to a friend who is a Christian, and start your journey of lifelong peace with Jesus. If you already believe in Christ, take time today to meditate on the amazing gift of "peace with God," which Jesus has accomplished for you.

PAUL

Peace in a New Identity

DAY 36

Peace When Your World Turns Upside-Down

Now as he went on his way, he approached Damascus, and suddenly a light from heaven shone around him. And falling to the ground, he heard a voice saying to him, "Saul, Saul, why are you persecuting me?" And he said, "Who are you, Lord?" And he said, "I am Jesus, whom you are persecuting."

Acts 9:3–5

• **Read Acts 9:1–22** •

Saul held the letters in his right hand tightly. Finally, *finally* he had the authority from the high priest to capture any followers of Jesus he found in Damascus and bring them back in chains to Jerusalem. He would be glad to rid the earth of those who declared that Jesus was the Messiah. *Wretched blasphemers!*

The dust on the road kicked up against his sandals as he walked. He sighed when he saw the outline of the city up ahead; their long journey was nearly over.

All at once, a light brighter than any sun shone around him, and Saul fell to the ground with a shudder. And then a voice, louder and stronger than any he could have imagined, resonated through him like a struck bell.

"Saul, Saul, why are you persecuting me?"

Sweat poured from his body—from heat or fear, he couldn't tell. Who was this? Could God be speaking to him? He flung his question into the light. "Who are you, Lord?"

That voice again, strong and unyielding, spoke into him. "I am Jesus, whom you are persecuting. But rise and enter the city, and you will be told what you are to do."

Saul felt as though he had been hit with a whip stronger than any made by human hands, so great was the blow to his heart and mind. *Jesus? How is it possible?*

He still couldn't see, blinded as he was by the light that had engulfed him. With his hands, he guided himself to his feet, willing his eyes to adjust. Willing his mind to adjust. *What must this mean?*

He kept blinking, but soon realized that the darkness around him was not dissipating. He yelled to the men he'd traveled with, although he didn't know if they were close or far off. "Can you see anything?"

Micah came up next to him and put a hand on his shoulder. "Yes, Saul. We can see just fine."

"Take me to Damascus, man. I need to get to the city. You'll . . . you'll have to lead me. I can't see."

His men secured lodgings for him at a house on Straight Street, and Saul asked to be left alone. He spent the days and nights fasting and praying. Although his physical blindness did not disappear, there in the darkness of his room in Damascus, Saul wept and prayed and asked the Lord for forgiveness. What had he been doing, persecuting believers? *Jesus was the Messiah.*

I remember the shock of waking up the morning after Michael proposed to me; I felt for my left hand in the dark, checking to see if a ring was still there, or if it had all been a dream. As I fingered the diamond while I lay in bed, I remember the sense of newness washing over me like a waterfall: Things were different now. I had agreed to marry Michael, and from here on out, our lives were going to be done together. This was a happy identity shift for me—but it was a shift, nonetheless. I started thinking about the future with both of us in mind. Soon I would be Ann *Swindell*, not Ann Taulbee. My identity and how I lived in the world was going to change.

Unlike the identity shift I was wading into, Saul's identity shift on the road to Damascus would not have been a happy one for him—at least not initially. He had built his career as a Pharisee in part by persecuting followers of Jesus, even standing by to watch Stephen's stoning—and approving of it (see Acts 7:58–8:1). He had been ravaging the church, barging into homes to carry believing men and women off to prison. He loved seeing Christians persecuted and punished (see Acts 8:3).

This is the man whom Jesus met in that bright light on the Damascus Road—a man full of hatred for Christians, a man who believed that he was upholding the ways of God by imprisoning those who followed Christ. When Jesus himself told Saul to stop persecuting him, Saul's entire world was turned upside-down.

In his days of blindness, the Lord revealed himself to Saul, and all of Saul's life—his training as a Pharisee, his persecution of believers—*all* of it was turned on its head. Saul rose from his blindness to be baptized, fully embracing the gospel that he had originally come to the city to try and destroy. And through Christ, Saul found peace with God.

> Your past identity is gone; you have peace with God through Christ.

Now that Saul understood and believed that Jesus was the Messiah, he was transformed from a persecutor of the church to its most fervent convert, "proclaim[ing] Jesus in the synagogues, saying, 'He is the Son of God'" (Acts 9:20). He repented of his sins and began the next chapter of his life as an evangelist for the Lord. The gospel changed his identity.

Saul's transformation was possible because he experienced the amazing truth of the gospel: that peace with God is available to all who believe in Christ. He knew himself to be a horrible sinner against Jesus—but he also knew the forgiveness of Jesus:

> Even though I was once a blasphemer and a persecutor and a violent man, I was shown mercy because I acted in ignorance and unbelief. The grace of our Lord was poured out on me abundantly, along with the faith and love that are in Christ Jesus.
>
> Here is a trustworthy saying that deserves full acceptance: Christ Jesus came into the world to save sinners—of whom I am the worst. But for that very reason I was shown mercy so that in me, the worst of sinners, Christ Jesus might display his immense patience as an example for those who would believe in him and receive eternal life. (1 Timothy 1:13–16 NIV)

If you have been saved by Christ, you have a new identity. You can respond like Saul by letting go of your past identity and choosing to cling solely to the gospel of Jesus today. You have been forgiven. Your past is gone; you have peace with God through Christ.

• **REFLECT:** Do you see yourself as a fully redeemed child of God? Like Saul, can you wholeheartedly rejoice in the grace, faith, and love that are in Christ Jesus that have been poured out on you? If not, perhaps there is something in your identity that you need to let go of—some old sin or way of thinking that doesn't line up with the gospel. Take time today to

ask the Lord to help you let go of things that don't line up with who you are as a new creation in Christ, and for the courage to walk forward in his peace.

DAY 37

Peace When Others Don't Believe You

And when he had come to Jerusalem, he attempted to join the disciples. And they were all afraid of him, for they did not believe that he was a disciple.

Acts 9:26

• Read Acts 9:22–31 •

Saul tried not to show his frustration. He had barely escaped from the Jews who were trying to kill him in Damascus for preaching the gospel. In fact, he had only made it out alive because one of his quick-witted disciples had the thought of lowering him over the city wall in a basket. It had been a perilous trip down; Saul had willed himself not to look.

His legs had been as soft as warm honey when he finally reached the ground, but he'd run as fast as he could toward Jerusalem. Now that he'd finally arrived, the followers of Jesus in the city didn't believe he was a genuine disciple.

He reminded himself *why* they didn't believe him—his reputation the last time he'd been here was as a persecutor of the church, not as an evangelist. Still, he was in earnest! He had changed!

At least Barnabas believed him. He was respected among the other believers, and for some reason—*praise the Lord Christ!*—he trusted Saul's story.

Which is why Saul now found himself standing in a room in front of Peter and John, two of the apostles. For the fourth time this week, Barnabas was relating Saul's Damascus Road story, along with the details of his baptism and preaching in Damascus. Earlier, Barnabas had told the story to rooms of disciples, encouraging them to believe that Saul was truly a brother in the faith. This time, in front of the apostles, Barnabas was less animated. He told the truth of the story without waiting for a response. Saul knew that he trusted the Holy Spirit to convince these men.

Saul's thoughts were interrupted by Peter. "Well, Saul. What do you have to say about Jesus for yourself?"

Saul's reply was immediate and assured. "That he is the Christ, the Messiah. That he was killed and rose again on the third day. That he lives and reigns and is coming back."

Peter looked to John, who nodded, and then back to Saul. "Welcome to our fellowship, brother. I must say—I never thought I would see you proclaiming his kingdom." He smiled, and then his smile turned pensive. "It would not be the first time I have been proven wrong."

John walked over to give Saul a loving embrace. "We are glad to count you as a brother in the faith. Preach the gospel. Do so in love."

Saul took a deep breath and nodded. "I will, brother John." It was the only thing he wanted to do.

Lord, let them see the truth.

I felt overwhelmed and didn't know what else to pray. The situation surrounding the loss of Michael's job hadn't been pretty, and I wasn't sure another church would be willing to take the risk of hiring us.

I deeply felt our need for the Holy Spirit to advocate for us. If Michael was ever going to get another pastoral position, we needed the Holy Spirit to reveal the truth to future employers. We knew that the more we tried to defend ourselves, the more we would seem desperate. God was going to have to pave the way for us.

Saul most definitely needed an advocate when he went to Jerusalem to find the Christians he had previously persecuted. His past made him an enemy of the church in the eyes of believers, and the Scriptures tell us that those in Jerusalem "did not believe that he was a disciple." How could he prove himself to them?

He didn't have to.

God advocated for him.

Saul's experience in Jerusalem is one that can give us hope—and peace. Why? Because the Lord did not leave him without an advocate in that city. For reasons the Scripture does not clarify, Barnabas believed Saul's story of transformation—and even stuck out his neck for him! As a respected believer in the community of Christians in Jerusalem (see Acts 4:36–37), Barnabas's words carried weight. He told Saul's story to the apostles and, by doing so, secured a place of trust for Saul in the greater community. And then? Saul started preaching the gospel boldly in Jerusalem. Even if there were still some believers in Jerusalem who were skeptical of his heart change, Saul

> We have the greatest Advocate in the person of the Holy Spirit.

didn't let that stop his kingdom work. He obeyed the Lord, did what he was called to do, and did so courageously.

God provided the advocate that Saul needed to do what he was called to do.

※

The Lord advocated for us too. In the middle of our interview process, God provided two friends who spoke up for us. One wrote a letter, and the other had a phone conversation with the lead pastor at the interviewing church.

More than anything else, though, the Holy Spirit moved in the hearts of the staff and elders at the church in Michigan, giving us favor with them. No earthly amount of self-defense or explanation could have created the supernatural grace that we experienced in that job interview process. Only the Lord could have accomplished that, and Michael was hired shortly thereafter.

※

When you find yourself needing someone to stick up for you, remember Saul's story and how God provided an advocate for him in Barnabas. And while the Lord may not always provide us with a human encourager to speak up for us, we have an even greater Advocate in the person of the Holy Spirit. Jesus spoke of him to the disciples:

> "And I will ask the Father, and he will give you another advocate to help you and be with you forever—the Spirit of truth. The world cannot accept him, because it neither sees him nor knows him. But you know him, for he lives with you and will be in you. . . .
>
> But the Advocate, the Holy Spirit, whom the Father will send in my name, will teach you all things and will remind you of everything I have said to you. Peace I leave with you; my peace I give you. I do not give to

you as the world gives. Do not let your hearts be troubled and do not be afraid" (John 14:16–17, 26–27 NIV).

Jesus clearly links the work of the Holy Spirit—our Advocate and Helper—to the peace that he gives to those who believe in him. For how can we not have peace when the very presence of Christ is within us? When we know that we are never alone, and that God himself is working on our behalf, we can have peace no matter what others say or think about us. We are accepted by God.

Saul did not have to defend himself; you do not have to defend yourself. As you continue to walk with Christ, the Holy Spirit will be your defender, your comforter, and your peace. You do not have to fight your own battles or make your own way. You do not have to walk in doubt or fear. You do not have to prove yourself. Walk faithfully with the Lord and trust that the greatest Advocate in the world is working on your behalf.

And let your soul be at rest.

- **REFLECT:** Is there any place in your heart where you feel like you have to prove yourself to others? Take that to the Lord today. Ask him to show you how he is already advocating for you and defending you, and ask him for the courage to stop trying to prove yourself. Rest in his love and peace instead.

DAY 38

Peace in Trial

*About midnight Paul and Silas were praying and singing
hymns to God, and the prisoners were listening to them, and
suddenly there was a great earthquake, so that the founda-
tions of the prison were shaken. And immediately all the doors
were opened, and everyone's bonds were unfastened.*

Acts 16:25–26

• **Read Acts 16:16–34** •

Paul tried to shift his back against the prison wall, but everything hurt.
It didn't matter how he moved—he would still be in pain.

His left eye was swollen shut, but he could still see through his right
eye, although it did him no good in the darkness. They had been put in
an inner cell, their feet locked in stocks. Paul leaned his head back. The
Philippians had given him and Silas a solid beating before tossing them
in jail, that was for sure. But they were alive, and for that, he was thankful.

Paul spoke into the darkness. "Silas? How are you?"

Silas grunted. "I've been better. But I don't think anything but my nose is broken. You?"

"My arm might be broken—I can't be sure. Other than that, just bruises and cuts, I think. And a nasty welt on my head."

Paul could hear the smile in his friend's voice. "The Lord has spared us, brother. I'm grateful."

Paul nodded and began to sing a hymn of gratitude to Jesus. Silas joined in. The presence of Christ was with them in their cell, and their hearts bubbled up with joy, singing and praying as the night wore on. As they spoke and sang their gratitude to their Lord, the pain of his bonds and beating faded in Paul's mind. *How good it was to belong to Christ!*

Without warning, the earth beneath him began rumbling—and then shaking—with a great pulsing that flowed through the jail like a wave. Paul tried to grasp for anything but found nothing to hold on to other than his own chains. Would the earthquake kill them or pass them by? But as the walls buckled, Paul felt the unexpected yet familiar peace of God flow through him. This was no earthly quaking—this was the Lord.

Paul heard the door to their cell fling open with a great whine just as the stocks released their pressure from his feet. God was freeing them!

The earth stopped its throbbing, and by the light of his torch, Paul saw their jailer look around wildly, noticing all the open doors and unchained prisoners. He reached for his sword and was about to deal himself the death stroke when Paul shouted at him.

"Do not harm yourself, for we are all here!"

Their jailer called to the others for light and then ran into their cell. The huge man fell at their feet, shaking with uncontained fear. Paul instinctively reached out to touch the man's head in kindness.

The jailer looked at the disciples with both wonder and worry, then hurried to help them up with a gentleness that surprised Paul. In the torchlight outside their cell, he spoke to them earnestly. "Sirs, what must I do to be saved?"

Paul smiled. Perhaps the Lord had brought them here for the salvation of this man. "Believe in the Lord Jesus and you will be saved, you and your household."

That very night, the jailer took Paul and Silas into his home and washed their wounds with his own hands and fed them from his own larder. As he cared for them, Paul and Silas shared the news of Jesus with him and his whole family, and all of them believed.

If there's one thing to be said about Paul's life as a follower of Jesus, it's that his life was never boring. (Now, as an evangelist to the Gentile world, Saul uses his Greek name—Paul—for the remainder of his ministry.) He was on the move much of the time, rarely staying in one place for very long. He saw people get saved, made new friends, took on new disciples, worked hard, and planted new churches. And his presence in many of the cities he traveled to caused an uproar. Both revivals and riots—these were common occurrences when Paul went into a city to preach the gospel.

Paul's experience in the city of Philippi is an example of this. He lands in the city and soon meets Lydia, who becomes the first Philippian convert. Things are off to a great start! However, shortly thereafter, Paul's rebuke of an evil spirit earns him and Silas a beating and imprisonment. The change of events is swift and painful. Suddenly, these men are seen as threats to the good of the city, and they don't know if their imprisonment will lead to more suffering or even to death.

God surprises them—and the entire prison—when he causes an earthquake that leads to their freedom, and also to the jailer's salvation. While it is a beautiful moment, it comes at great personal cost to Paul. He was severely beaten and treated horribly. His future is in limbo. His friend, Silas, is also suffering.

And yet the Scriptures show us that Paul is, amazingly, at peace throughout the entire ordeal. Although they are battered and wounded, Paul and Silas use their time in the darkness of prison to worship God through song and prayer, singing so loudly that the rest of the prisoners and jailers hear their words. They know that their lives are in God's hands, and so they worship the Lord for who he is, even in the middle of an awful situation.

Years later, Paul writes a letter to the Philippian church, thanking them for their care, and perhaps also remembering his time in their jail:

> I have learned in whatever situation I am to be content. I know how to be brought low, and I know how to abound. In any and every circumstance, I have learned the secret of facing plenty and hunger, abundance and need. I can do all things through him who strengthens me. (Philippians 4:11–13)

Paul is a disciple who has learned to be content, no matter what he faces. Whether he has much or little, whether he is exalted or disparaged, he is *at peace in Christ*. He has what he needs because he has Jesus. His strength to endure everything from prison to plenty comes from the fact that he is united to Christ.

As we choose the way of Christ, we will find the peace that passes understanding and overcomes anxiety.

All of us, like Paul, will face highs and lows, joy and sorrow. He was a human being like us. Yes, God set him apart for his unique ministry on earth, but Paul was not a superhero. He had to learn to be content—he had to *learn* how to find peace in Christ in whatever circumstance he faced.

The same is true for us. Most of us will not automatically find ourselves singing hymns in the lowest moments of our days—but we can *learn* to do so. Most of us will not knee-jerk our way into prayer when our bodies or minds are hurting—but we can *learn* to do so. We can train our hearts, through practice and time, to turn to Jesus in our pain rather than wallowing in it.

We can choose to open the Bible rather than scrolling on our phones.

We can choose to turn on a worship song rather than the TV.

We can choose to call a friend and ask for prayer rather than calling to gripe.

These are not easy choices, but they are choices, nonetheless. As we choose the way of Christ over our flesh, we will find the peace that passes understanding and overcomes anxiety. Paul wrote about this in the same letter to the Philippians:

> The Lord is at hand; do not be anxious about anything, but in everything by prayer and supplication with thanksgiving let your requests be made known to God. And the peace of God, which surpasses all understanding, will guard your hearts and your minds in Christ Jesus. (Philippians 4:5–7)

What Paul did in that jail cell—offering prayer and thanksgiving to Christ—*that* is how we learn the secret of facing anything that comes our way. For as we do so, God's peace will guard us, no matter where we are.

• **REFLECT:** How can you make the choice to learn to be content in Christ today? How can you offer him prayer and thanksgiving in the midst of your own trials, knowing that as you do, his peace will guard your heart? Ask him to help you make choices today that lead to peace in him.

DAY 39

Peace in Embracing Weakness

*Therefore I will boast all the more gladly of my weaknesses,
so that the power of Christ may rest upon me. For the sake of Christ,
then, I am content with weaknesses, insults, hardships, persecutions, and calamities. For when I am weak, then I am strong.*

2 Corinthians 12:9–10

● **Read 2 Corinthians 11:22–30 and 12:1–10** ●

Paul knew he needed to write a letter to the Corinthian church. He was worried they were being led astray from the purity of their first love to Christ! So-called "super apostles" had come to them, and the Corinthians were attracted to their prestige and accolades. Unfortunately, the Corinthians had started to listen to them—and they didn't preach Christ in truth.

How to remind them of the treasure of Jesus?

How to prove to them that the message they'd heard from him was the true gospel?

He felt the stirring of the Holy Spirit in his heart, drawing his mind off of himself and to his King. *If they want prestige and accolades, I'm going to have to boast to win them back,* Paul thought. *Then I will boast!* He smiled. *But I will boast of my weakness—and give all the glory to Jesus.*

He let his mind wander back across the years he had been Christ's bondservant. There had been so many beatings, too many to count. He'd hung in the space between life and death more than he could remember, pulled back to life in the body only because Jesus had more work for him to do.

Then there'd been the stoning, and that time he'd been lost at sea for a full day . . . *Oh! One, two, three shipwrecks.* He was often traveling, often in danger from thieves and false brothers, often hungry and cold, often short on sleep. But the thing that worried him above all else? His fear that the believers—like those at the church in Corinth—would fall away from Christ.

Yes. *If I must boast, I will boast of the things that show my weakness. I'll tell them about my physical agony, and the prayer for healing that the Lord refuses to answer for me.*

But he would share the Lord's words too, and then perhaps they'd remember that weakness in Christ was better than any so-called human accolades. The false apostles might offer them a smooth story . . . but they could not offer the truth of Jesus.

He started composing the letter in his head. *But the Lord said to me, "My grace is sufficient for you, for my power is made perfect in weakness." Therefore, I will boast all the more gladly of my weaknesses, so that the power of Christ may rest upon me. For the sake of Christ, then, I am content with weaknesses, insults, hardships, persecutions, and calamities. For when I am weak, then I am strong. . . .*

I spend very little time boasting about my weaknesses. In fact, I usually try to ignore my weaknesses as much as possible. Take for example, my lack of sense of direction. I have absolutely zero sense of direction. In the years before maps were readily available on our phones, I had to write out painstakingly clear directions before making any new journey in the car. (*Turn left at Main Street, drive past three roads, take a sharp right onto Washington.*) Even now, if the map's function on my phone isn't connecting or is too slow to load, I panic. I often have no idea where I am.

Directions notwithstanding, I have plenty of other weaknesses. I've struggled with a hair-pulling condition called trichotillomania for over twenty years. I have an inclination toward anxiety and worry that can leave me feeling overwhelmed with fear about what I can't control. I'm cranky toward those I love the most when I'm tired, and I worry too much about what others think of me. Left unchecked, some of these weaknesses become sin. But many of them are just realities that I deal with because of the nature and nurture of my life.

And that's just scratching the surface.

We all have weaknesses that we deal with on a regular basis. Whether they're physical weaknesses, emotional weaknesses, or relational ones, all of us know what it's like to feel that we just can't get past what holds us back. *If only*, we think. *If only* we could lose ten pounds. *If only* we could have more energy. *If only* we could stop reaching for the cigarette, or the chocolate bar, or the soda. *If only* our temper wasn't so short. *If only* we were more athletic.

What's so startling and beautiful about Paul's letter to the church in Corinth is that he turns his weaknesses on their head. He was writing to a culture where power and prestige were highly valued (sound familiar?), and the believers there were being pulled astray from the true gospel to another message that didn't uphold Christ. Paul was desperate to win them back, and he knew that he needed to speak into their culture. However, rather than share the many (many!) accolades he could have written about (see Philippians 3), Paul instead draws their attention to the countless ways that he has been battered and bruised for the gospel. He points them to the inverted truth of the kingdom of God: our weaknesses are gateways for the strength of Christ to shine.

Paul writes that "For the sake of Christ, I am content with weaknesses, insults, hardships, persecutions, and calamities" (2 Corinthians 12:10). Paul is a man at peace with his struggles and pains.

Why?

Because Christ's power is made perfect—his power is accomplished—in our weakness.

> **Our weaknesses are the doorway for Christ's power and glory to be displayed.**

Our weaknesses are the doorway for Christ's power and glory to enter in and be displayed.

Christ, rather than being dismayed by our weaknesses, draws himself close to us in our struggles and trials.[1] He meets us in those places of powerlessness and frailty, and shows himself to be our strength and our portion.

When you butt up against your weaknesses and your heart feels anxious, remember Paul. In your weakness, Christ is strong. In your places of struggle, God's grace is sufficient for you. When you feel like your peace is gone and your heart is failing, lean in to the Scripture:

> My flesh and my heart may fail, but God is the strength of my heart and my portion forever. (Psalm 73:26)

Be at peace. Though all you can feel is weakness, God is your strength. God is giving you grace, and God's power is going to be displayed in your life.

---

1. For an in-depth look at this beautiful truth, read Dane Ortlund's book *Gentle and Lowly: The Heart of Christ for Sinners and Sufferers* (Wheaton: Crossway, 2020).

- **REFLECT:** How can you boast in your weakness today? Start by thanking the Lord for the weak places in your life—and then ask him to show his glory through you in those areas. You don't have to be strong; your soul can rest in Christ's strength instead.

DAY 40

Peace When Christ Is
Your Greatest Treasure

*But I do not account my life of any value nor as precious to myself,
if only I may finish my course and the ministry that I received
from the Lord Jesus, to testify to the gospel of the grace of God.*

Acts 20:24

• Read Acts 20:17–24 •

Paul was tired. He'd traveled to Macedonia, Greece, back to Macedonia, then to Troas, and to Assos. Then, by boat, they'd been to Mitylene, Chios, Samos, and now they were in Miletus. He wanted to try and reach Jerusalem by the day of Pentecost, although he wasn't sure if he would make it.

But first, he had a message to give to the elders of the church at Ephesus. He sent a man across the sixty-three miles to get to them, knowing it would be days before they all arrived. He spent the time in prayer and preparation. Yes, he was going to Jerusalem.

When the men arrived, exhausted from the journey they'd made in haste, Paul embraced them as the brothers they were. *So many faithful men.* He asked about the church in Ephesus, and was heartened to learn that there were many continuing to follow the Lord.

"Come, friends." Paul gathered the elders around him to share what he knew they did not want to hear.

"Behold, I am going to Jerusalem, constrained by the Spirit, not knowing what will happen to me there, except that the Holy Spirit testifies to me in every city that imprisonment and afflictions await me."

"No!" Tears started coursing down Alexios's face. "Do not leave us, Paul!"

Paul shook his head. "I do not account my life of any value nor as precious to myself, if only I may finish my course and the ministry that I received from the Lord Jesus, to testify to the gospel of the grace of God."

Several other men nodded, although Alexios was not the only one with tears in his eyes anymore.

Paul took a deep breath. This would be the hardest for them. "And now, behold, I know that none of you among whom I have gone about proclaiming the kingdom will see my face again." Jerome and Gregor gasped, but Paul continued on: "Therefore I testify to you this day that I am innocent of the blood of all of you, for I did not shrink from declaring to you the whole counsel of God. Pay careful attention to yourselves and to all the flock, of which the Holy Spirit has made you overseers, to care for the church of God, which he obtained with his own blood."

There were tears in Paul's own eyes now, for he knew that Satan was relentless in trying to destroy the church. Oh, how he longed for these believers to stay faithful!

Paul held out his hands to them in blessing. "And now I commend you to God and to the word of his grace, which is able to build you up and to give you the inheritance among all those who are sanctified."

Then Paul knelt to pray with these precious brothers, and they all wept together, embracing one another and memorizing each other's faces. This would be the last time he would see them—the Lord had made that clear.

Paul looked at the sun and knew it was time. The elders, unwilling to leave him yet, walked with him to the ship. He waved good-bye from the bow as the boat pulled from port, a prayer on his lips. *Lord, help them remain faithful to you.*

⚬

By the time Paul sailed for Jerusalem, he knew that what was ahead for him was imprisonment and affliction, and that when he left his beloved brothers from Ephesus, he would never see them on earth again. It would be easy to imagine that Paul might have been filled with anxiety—he was headed toward trouble. And yet he did not hesitate to go; the Scriptures, in fact, are clear that he was in a rush to get to Jerusalem, hastening to get there quickly (see Acts 20:16).

How could Paul, who knew that all that was ahead of him were trial and tribulation, go forward in such confidence and peace?

He could go in peace because Paul's greatest treasure was not his own life. His greatest treasure was the Lord Jesus:

> But I do not account my life of any value nor as precious to myself, if only I may finish my course and the ministry that I received from the Lord Jesus, to testify to the gospel of the grace of God. (Acts 20:24)

All that Paul longed to do was to be faithful to the course God had set him on—to share the "gospel of the grace" and to complete the work he was put on earth to do.

This is a theme in Paul's life—that of counting Jesus more precious than himself. Although he had many reasons to count his own life as precious because of his lineage, his education, and his intelligence, he instead counted it as *nothing* compared to Jesus:

> But whatever gain I had, I counted as loss for the sake of Christ. Indeed, I count everything as loss because of the surpassing worth of knowing Christ Jesus my Lord. For his sake I have suffered the loss of all things and count them as rubbish, in order that I may gain Christ and be found in him, not having a righteousness of my own that comes from the law, but that which comes through faith in Christ, the righteousness from God that depends on faith—that I may know him and the power of his resurrection, and may share his sufferings, becoming like him in his death, that by any means possible I may attain the resurrection from the dead. (Philippians 3:7–11)

Compared to Jesus, Paul says that everything—*absolutely everything else*—is rubbish. Paul eventually lost everything for Jesus, but to him the trade-off was never in question.

Christ was his greatest treasure.

Christ was his deepest joy.

Christ was everything to Paul, and so losing his life was a minuscule price to pay in order to have Jesus in exchange.

There is peace in knowing that Christ can never be taken away from us!

Oh, that we might be like our brother Paul! This is the reason that he was able to walk in peace, regardless of circumstance. This is the reason he could face any trial and have a soul at rest. This is the reason—*Christ was his greatest treasure!* Everything else paled in comparison to Jesus! Paul wrote, "For to me to live is Christ, and to die is gain" (Philippians 1:21). He *longed* to be with Jesus.

When we long for Christ more than anything else, we can always have his peace. When we desire Christ more than life, his peace will never be hard to find. For Christ can never be taken away from us. We may lose our homes, our jobs, our family, our friends, and even our very lives—but we will *never* lose Jesus. Christ himself declares this wonderful truth:

> "All that the Father gives me will come to me, and whoever comes to me I will never cast out. For I have come down from heaven, not to do my own will but the will of him who sent me. And this is the will of him who sent me, that I should lose nothing of all that he has given me, but raise it up on the last day. For this is the will of my Father, that everyone who looks on the Son and believes in him should have eternal life, and I will raise him up on the last day" (John 6:37–40).

Christ will never lose us. We will never lose him. And so our souls can be at rest, for our greatest prize and most wonderful treasure will never be lost to us.

Jesus is ours.

We are his.

All is well.

• **REFLECT:** Is Christ your greatest treasure? Is there anything other than Christ that holds that place in your heart? Ask the Lord to help you desire him more than anything else, and let your soul be at peace in him as you cling to the beautiful truth that you can never lose Jesus. He will always hold on to you.

FINAL THOUGHTS

Peace in Unfulfilled Longings

Life on this broken earth means that each of us will wrestle with unfulfilled longings. Each of us will feel the ache for something better and easier and more wonderful than what we have right now. Regardless of what our longing is for—perhaps a spouse, a home, a child, a friend, a job—we all know the subtle ache that can linger just below the surface of our minds. That ache whispers that things here aren't good enough, or that they aren't satisfying. The lie that can easily slip in is that the life we have been given is second-rate or that we have been looked over by God and others.

The truth? Things here *aren't* ultimately satisfying. They *aren't* good enough—not for us or for anyone. There is not a human on the planet—from the poorest soul to the richest celebrity—who hasn't felt the pang of disappointment and yearning. The longings that we feel here on earth for things to be *well* and *right* and *good* are longings that will never be fully met in our days on this soil.

Why? Because what we are truly longing for is heaven. We long for unity with Christ himself.

All of the men and women we have studied in this book—Sarah, Moses, Ruth, Hannah, Mary, the disciples, Mary Magdalene, Paul—every one of them had their own longings that were met in part (but not in full) here on earth. Sarah and Hannah were given children; Ruth was provided for. Moses saw the freedom of his people; Mary saw the resurrection of her son and Savior, the Christ. The disciples experienced Jesus' miracles and listened to his teachings. Mary Magdalene was set free from oppression; Paul was set free from his spiritual blindness. These are beautiful and wonderful parts of their stories, but it was still not enough; they were men and women like you and me. They had the same aching longing for perfection and wholeness and abundant life. And those who lived before Jesus' life, death, and resurrection lived by faith, trusting that they would one day experience all that God had promised them.

The book of Hebrews shares about how these saints lived on earth:

> These all died in faith, not having received the things promised, but having seen them and greeted them from afar, and having acknowledged that they were strangers and exiles on the earth. For people who speak thus make it clear that they are seeking a homeland. If they had been thinking of that land from which they had gone out, they would have had opportunity to return. But as it is, they desire a better country, that is, a heavenly one. Therefore God is not ashamed to be called their God, for he has prepared for them a city. (Hebrews 11:13–16)

These men and women ached for heaven. They longed for it with all their hearts. And Sarah and Moses and Ruth and Hannah died before the Messiah came. Still, they trusted God, who was able to carry all their longings even as he prepared for them a heavenly city. They died without knowing what was ahead, but they had faith in God and followed him anyway.

Mary and the disciples, Mary Magdalene, and Paul—these men and women lived through the grace of Jesus living and dying and rising again. They knew Jesus and were some of the first saints to experience the fulfillment of the promise that God completed in the Messiah. Their longing for heaven was both met and awakened in the person of Christ. And the gift of the Holy Spirit, given after his ascension (see Acts 2:1–4), sustained their work and witness until they each finished their own race on earth.

And us? We also have the incredible gift of the indwelling of the Holy Spirit—the very Spirit of Christ with us forever (see Galatians 4:6). We will never be alone; we are not spiritual orphans in this broken world (see John 14:15–18). Christ is with us now. Any unmet longing we have can be brought to him in prayer, where his Holy Spirit will meet us and comfort us until the day when all of our longings will be fulfilled in heaven.

Will we escape hardship and suffering because we are followers of Christ? No. Will that ache for something better—something perfect— ever leave us? Not on this earth. Our souls know that heaven is where we belong. And although we cannot always name the pangs of yearning that we feel for something better, we *can* let them draw us to Christ. We can allow our desires for a better life and a perfect existence to draw our hearts to the best and most perfect one: Jesus.

For if we don't allow our yearnings to draw us to Christ, the alternative is a life full of fear and worry. If we don't give our unfulfilled longings to Jesus, we will constantly live with the anxiety that we are missing out on what we think we should have, or that we are somehow getting cheated out of the best of life.

The opposite is actually true: The best of life is yet to come. Not here, but in heaven. So we can let Christ—the Prince of Peace—comfort us here, while we simultaneously allow the longing for heaven and union with him to draw us closer to his Word and to his heart.

As we meet with Jesus through his Word, in prayer, and by being in Christian community through his Church, we will find that he meets our unmet longings with himself. We are not always given what we want here on earth; what we are given is more of Christ.

And he is more than enough. The saints who have gone before us declare with their lives that Christ is the greatest prize and the highest treasure.

This is ultimately what unfulfilled longings are meant for—they are meant to draw us to the One who will fulfill every longing and fill every empty cup. As we live and work and love here on earth with longings that are yet unmet, we can ask our Lord and Savior to meet us with his love that satisfies us, with his presence that sustains us—and with his peace that comforts us.

And one day, when we see him face-to-face, every longing we have will be completely met in him.

Acknowledgments

To Jeff, Deirdre, Jennifer, Amanda, and the whole team at Bethany House—thank you for your belief in this project and in me. I'm grateful to do kingdom ministry with you!

To my Writing with Grace Mastermind women: I'm so proud of each of you for walking with Christ and writing with and for him. Partnering with you is one of my greatest joys.

To Jen and Ryan: lifelong friends and disciples of Christ. You live out this message of walking in Christ's peace, and we are so thankful for you.

To Claire and Wade: you are both family *and* friends. Love you.

To my parents: Thank you for always being a safe place to land, and for making it possible for me to chase after Christ's call on my life. You are the best, and I love you both so much!

To Ella and Judah: You are treasures from God, and being your mama is an immeasurable gift. Thank you for cheering me on in my writing. I love you both more than you will ever know!

To Michael, my biggest supporter: Thank you for loving me and helping me do the work God has called me to do. You always lead me to Jesus; I am so grateful, and I love you.

To the Lord Almighty, my Savior and King: My life is for you! May you be glorified in every way through my words, my heart, and my life.

ANN SWINDELL is a writer and speaker who is committed to seeing women set free by the truth and love of Christ. She is the author of *The Path to Peace* (Bethany House, 2022) and *Still Waiting* (Tyndale, 2017), and her work has been featured in *The Gospel Coalition*, *Risen Motherhood*, *Desiring God*, *Deeply Rooted*, and *(in)courage*, along with multiple devotionals and anthologies. She is joyfully married to Michael, and they are raising their kids in Michigan, where he is a pastor. Ann loves helping other writers share their stories beautifully and powerfully through her ministries, *Writing with Grace* and *The Writing Mom Course*. You can get to know her more at AnnSwindell.com.